God Is Greater

God Is Greater

Theology for the World

Antje Jackelén

Fortress Press
Minneapolis

GOD IS GREATER
Theology for the World

Print ISBN: 978-1-5064-6051-2
eBook ISBN: 978-1-5064-6052-9

Copyright © 2020 Fortress Press. All rights reserved. Except for brief quotations in critical articles or reviews, no part of this book may be reproduced in any manner without prior written permission from the publisher. Email copyright@1517.media or write to Permissions, Fortress Press, PO Box 1209, Minneapolis, MN 55440-1209.

Unless otherwise noted, Scripture quotations are from the New Revised Standard Version Bible, © 1989 by the Division of Christian Education of the National Council of the Churches of Christ in the USA and used by permission. All rights reserved.

Cover design: Laurie Ingram
Cover image: © iStock 2019; Beach with sun stock photo by plusphoto.

Contents

	Preface	*vii*
1.	Critical Solidarity: The Place of the Church Is in the Midst of the World	*1*
2.	After Secularization: The Time for Simple Explanations Is Past	*60*
3.	Beyond the Caricatures: The Future Requires Well-Functioning Interplay between Faith and Science	*111*
4.	Cosmic Passion History: In a Complex World Evil Has Several Roles	*167*
5.	Be Grounded in Grace, Create in the World	*218*

Questions for Reflection and Conversation	*257*
Sources and References	*264*

Preface

Religion is here to stay. In spite of secularization and a decrease in religious affiliation in some regions of the world, the global picture is different. Religious "nones," including people who identify as atheist or agnostic, as well as those who have no particular religion, are declining on a global level. And, notably, this is a trend that is supposed to last for several decades. According to the Pew Research Center, by 2055 to 2060, just 9 percent of all babies will be born to religiously unaffiliated women, while more than seven-in-ten will be born to either Muslims (36 percent) or Christians (35 percent).[1]

1. http://www.pewforum.org/2017/04/05/the-changing-global-religious-landscape/

PREFACE

All major issues in politics and society have religious and spiritual dimensions. In other words, they benefit from theological analysis. This book contributes to such analysis and reflection. It is indeed exciting to be able to present *God Is Greater* for an English-speaking audience! I wish to express my sincere gratitude to translators and editors.

Five Poisonous P's

In all too many countries these days, people are constantly drinking from a cocktail made of five dangerous ingredients, five poisonous P's: polarization, populism, protectionism, post-truth, and patriarchy. These poisons affect science, religion, and society. Polarization tears apart what should belong together and work together. Populism pits people and so-called elites against each other. Protectionism puts one's own country, one's own people, and one's own interests first, at the expense of the common good. Post-truth is the contempt of truth that disfigures the vital triad of the true, the good, and the beautiful, without which we cannot live. Patriarchy continues to deprive the world of the full flourishing of women and children, and in the end, it dehumanizes men as well as women.

I do not know a panacea that will make this drunken world sober and whole. However, literacy certainly is a key element in countering the worst consequences. We need literacy in science, philosophy (hermeneutics!), and theology (factual knowledge as well as spiritual practice and experience). We know from history how much literacy has meant for the development of societies, especially the literacy of girls and women.

Social media has facilitated communication between people significantly. At the same time, the pace of this new communication often counteracts careful reflection. Extreme positions make themselves heard louder and louder, and the risk is that the extremes will silence the mainstream—the margins marginalize the middle, as it were.

Migration has become one of the major issues of our time. There is much to suggest that we have entered a prolonged period of relatively major global migration caused by conflicts, climate change, and other geopolitical factors. In its wake, many well-tested systems might appear as more fragile than expected. Social cohesion within the immediate community, as well as agents in civil society, become increasingly important for sustaining social well-being.

An increasing presence of religion in the cultural

debate as well as in politics at the local, national, and international levels comes with new requirements. For example, skills in interfaith dialogue are important for peace—in the village as well as in the world. Therefore, it is important that education give young people a fair picture of what it means to have a religious faith. Education that conveys the impression that faith belongs in the past, consists of strange teachings and practices, and is something that only "the others" engage in, will block their understanding of the existential power of faith and will leave them ill equipped to meet the challenges of life in the world today and in the future.

God Is Greater

The title of this book is also the motto I adopted when I was consecrated as bishop in 2007: "God is greater," a quote from 1 John 3:18–20. It has proven to be an excellent conversation starter. The idea that this motto implies both trust and a challenge has obviously fitted many people's experience very well. The knowledge that God is greater than our best achievements and our worst failures creates, on the one hand, space for relaxation and a sense of humor. On the other hand, this same knowledge protects us against arrogance and creates a healthy humility: God is greater than all our ideas about God, and today's answers will be tested by tomorrow's questions.

The insight that the Christian confession that God is greater overlaps with the Muslim *Allahu akbar* (which is "God is greater" in Arabic) has given rise to some interesting discussions about how religions relate to one another. Jews, Christians, and Muslims are united in their faith in God, the Creator of the universe. Even when we speak of the Holy Spirit as God's creative power, we can find much in common with people of other faiths. It is when it comes to Jesus Christ that we differ. A Jew can happily and proudly see that the Jew Jesus is at the center of the church. A Muslim has great respect for Jesus as one of the most important prophets—a respect that is also expressed in the Qur'an. But it is only we Christians who believe that Jesus is the Son of God and the savior of the world. As Christians, we can be clear about our faith in Jesus Christ and at the same time respect other people's faith.

However, during the last six years or so, some conversations about "God is greater changed." They shifted from the biblical and Christian context into polemics directed against Islam in general and the

PREFACE

abuse of the Muslim confession in connection with acts of violence and terrorism in particular. A number of critics did not know that the biblical texts are at least six hundred years older than those of the Qur'an. For far too many people, the distinction between Islam and terrorism in the name of Islam dwindled away completely.

Abuse of words and symbols has also affected Christianity. Crime committed in the name of God marks a dark streak in the ongoing history of the world's religions. And if this abuse is allowed to destroy the good use of words, symbols, and rites, then evil will have won the day.

The motto "God is greater" is deeply rooted both in the Bible and in the Christian tradition. In its Latin translation, *Deus (semper) maior*, this phrase can be found, for example, in the writings of Augustine (354–430), Anselm of Canterbury (1033–1109), and Ignatius of Loyola (1491–1556). In John 14:28 Jesus himself says, "The Father is greater than I am." In the book of Job we read that God is greater than human beings (33:12) and that God is greater than we can understand: the number of God's years is unsearchable (36:26).

This book, which originally matured during my time as bishop of the Diocese of Lund, Sweden, has been enriched by insights from my time as archbishop, but experiences from my time as parish priest in the dioceses of Stockholm and Lund as well as from my years as teaching theologian at Lund University and the Lutheran School of Theology at Chicago have also contributed to it. While many examples refer to a Swedish or European context, I hope that they will prove meaningful even for international readers, since the experience of familiarity as well as that of strangeness can broaden our understanding of our own home turf. The chapters can be read in any order of choice.

Encountering the God who is greater than our best achievements and our worst failures is an encounter with grace. I hope and pray that every reader will be uplifted by that encounter. The discovery of the grace that liberates us gives us an appetite for life that is greater than our fear that things might go wrong—so that, in Martin Luther's words, our heart will jump and dance in the great joy that God gives us.

Antje Jackelén
The Archbishop's Residence, Uppsala
Pentecost 2019

1

Critical Solidarity: The Place of the Church Is in the Midst of the World

A summer Saturday in Yogyakarta, Indonesia: Some fifty women and men have gathered for a day seminar on science and faith. About two-thirds are Muslim, and one-third Christian. It is hard to tell who is what. Some are students from the city; others have traveled for eight hours in order to participate. I know almost nothing about the conditions of a student or a professor in Yogyakarta, and to them, a female bishop from a Christian church somewhere in northern Europe is probably a very rare phenomenon. Our group of visitors consists of eight scientists and theologians from Australia, France, the United States, and Sweden. In spite of all the strangeness, this exchange feels deeply meaningful. There is intensive listening, and the students ask important questions. We learn from one another. For us foreigners, it is most educational when the Indonesians discuss among themselves.

During the break we hear about a recently started international research program for intercultural studies. This program is a unique collaboration between three universities in Yogyakarta—one national-secular university, one Muslim university, and one Christian university. The director of studies, the Islamologist Fatimah Husein, is enthusiastic about the start of the first course, which has seventeen PhD students. A sign of hope—because there are conflicts between the Muslim majority and the Christian minority in the largest Muslim country in the world.

In the evening, our little Western group gathers at a Jesuit convent. We celebrate mass in a simple chapel, sitting barefoot in the tropical heat. As we belong to different churches—including some that do not officially have intercommunion with one another—we experience the mystery of faith all the more richly as we unite in prayer and Eucharist. At that moment, we constitute one of those pockets where eucharistic hospitality is practiced with humility and respect while yearning for the day when it will become officially possible. From outside, we hear some of the innumerable motorbikes in this city. Our prayers are mingled with the sound of the Muslim prayer calls that reach us through the open windows.

The Gospel that evening tells the story of the woman who anointed the feet of Jesus, kissed them, and wiped them with her hair; of Simon, who complained that this was unsuitable; and of Jesus, who corrected Simon, who was so sure of how things ought to be (Luke 19). The preacher, a Dominican, points out how truth, compassion, and empathy belong together.

The impressions of the day blend together: the intellectual curiosity that engaged us across so many boundaries, the enthusiasm for collaboration between religions for the sake of the people and the world, and the encounter with the God who is greater than all those boundaries on which we sometimes make ourselves far too dependent.

The church lives "in the world" in a double sense—in the local society and in the global world. The church was a globalized movement long before the word *globalization* had been coined. Through mission, aid, and participation in colonization, the church had gained both good and less-good experiences of the global world long before the world economy began to take note of the advantages and disadvantages of globalization.

The Parish Hall at the small town of Vittsjö in the north of the province of Skåne in Sweden is decorated by an imaginative mural from 1970 by David Ralson, which captures a picture of the globalization perspective of the late nineteenth century. The painting shows village life at Vittsjö united with village life in Africa on one and the same wall. Contemporary scenes from everyday life, including work, teaching and nurture, care, and technological development are held together through biblical symbols and motifs. At the center is found the tree of life, shaped as a cross with a crown of thorns that grows out into a crown of leaves, and the leaves provide "healing for the peoples" (Rev 22:2).

During the twentieth century, global relationships have developed with increasing emphasis on mutuality and partnership. Today, this shapes the work of organizations such as the Lutheran World Federation, the World Council of Churches, and the ACT Alliance—an alliance of more than 150 churches and faith-based organizations that work to provide humanitarian aid and development. Collaboration between the churches, development aid work, and advocacy—to argue in favor of and working for social justice on various issues—do of course have political dimensions. The churches have a critical and self-critical responsibility that can lead to socio-political consequences. This became particularly obvious in connection with the international efforts made by many churches in the fight against apartheid in South Africa.

At the home scene, the presence of the church in society finds many different expressions. Besides what happens in the church's own localities, the church is also present through the professional work of priests, deacons, musicians, educational and other church staff members in workplaces, hospitals, prisons, special care homes, schools, and the like. This takes place through collaboration with other social functions, such as crisis work, psychological and social care in situations of crisis, and in various forums for dialogue. But above all, this takes place primarily through the fact that members of the church are a major part of society. The Christian church, regardless of which denomination, does not become present only when an employed church worker turns up but is almost always already there. Through every baptized person, the church is physically present in the world. Nevertheless, it is this form of presence that in Swedish society has been made most invisible, since here few dogmas are followed as faithfully as the belief that faith is a private matter.

God's presence is sought not only when people gather in church buildings or participate in church activities. It is part of the Christian faith to believe and expect that God's love and care will also be expressed in society at large, in and through our worldly ordinances.

Touching Generates Warmth

Inspired by the German philosopher and sociologist Georg Simmel (1858–1918), bishop Mikael Mogren (b. 1969) pointed out the difference between society and sociability. Here society refers to institutions and structures—to everything that is governed by laws and economy. Sociability, on the other hand, refers to the social capital, the relationships that are created between people—to everything that makes people experience community and friendship, particularly to everything that cannot be measured by money. Sociability is built on interaction and mutuality. That makes it possible to have someone to call when you hear of something nice, or to have a meal together, as Mogren puts it.

In Sweden we have quite a lot of society and less sociability. Things are well organized and regulated through and through. If everyone sticks to the rules, no real collisions need to occur. We can pass one another by without meeting one another's eyes. We can glide past one another without any congestion or any need for confrontation. Quite often our social life runs on without any friction, and that certainly has its advantages. And disadvantages! Friction generates warmth. Wherever touching becomes superfluous, there will be less warmth. Society becomes somewhat colder.

Since 1995 the Diocese of Lund has had a link diocese in Southern Sudan (since 2011 in South Sudan) called the Diocese of Lui. Women and men from South Sudan have visited Sweden, and groups from the Diocese of Lund have visited the Diocese of Lui on several occasions—both "at home" in South Sudan and in the South Sudanese refugee congregations that used to exist in the Khartoum area. Due to many years of war and poverty, the infrastructure in South Sudan is very weak—at least to Western eyes. Medical care, education, and church are areas where not much society can be seen, but sociability can be seen all the more. A church custom that I have experienced several times in South Sudan has become a powerful symbol of this. After the service, the priests go outside into the church yard. The congregation follows and stands around in a semi-circle, and everyone greets everyone else while there is singing and dancing. Everyone from the youngest to the oldest, the weakest and the strongest, the cleanest and the dirtiest—all are included. The handshakes feel different; the faces show traces of various life experiences. None of us visitors can speak the local Moro language, but we somehow manage to meet without words.

There is great poverty in South Sudan. And there is great joy. Far be it from me to romanticize poverty. There is nothing romantic whatsoever in the fact that the hospital in Lui could diagnose HIV but did not have access to any anti-retroviral medicines at all when I was there in 2008.

I do however see a connection between sociability and joy. A high degree of sociability furthers friendship and joy. A high degree of society is focused on the rights and obligations of the individual as they emerge from the relevant rules and regulations. Sociability needs some help to get going in society. The church is well placed to contribute toward a good balance between sociability and society.

It often seems as if sociability works better abroad than at home. In Lui it was quite easy for Swedes and South Sudanese to find one another in the Christian faith, in prayer, song, and dance, in spite of the language difficulties, in spite of the circumstances that were so incredibly different, and even in spite of the fact that theology and liturgy differ between our churches. There was, however, a tangible recognition that we were all sisters and brothers in the human and Christian community. Why is this easier in South Sudan than at home?

Individuality is important, but it is not sufficient for a flourishing society. It is not individuality but community that is the foundation for our lives. Our life emerges from community, it is nourished by community, and it contributes to community—even when we live alone. When individuality is asserted at the cost of community, all focus falls on individual rights and possible offenses against them. This easily pulls a gloomy veil of melancholy over life and community.

Cultural melancholy is a worrying phenomenon. It

can spread like a virus throughout our entire society—through newspapers, on TV and the internet, and in schools, politics, caring institutions, churches, voluntary organizations, and families. We cannot vaccinate ourselves against all the attacks of cultural melancholy. But we are not helpless victims either. We can influence the relationship between sociability and society—at least in our own local area.

Love Life, Hate the Law of Jante

(Translator's note: The law of Jante is used as a description of a pattern of group behavior toward individuals within Scandinavian communities that negatively portrays and criticizes individual success and achievement as unworthy and inappropriate. It is linked to a condescending attitude toward individual success: "Don't pretend you are somebody!")

"Young in the Worldwide Church" is a grants program that makes it possible for young Christians to gather valuable experience from abroad. For example, Swedish youngsters have traveled to Brazil and Costa Rica, and Swedish parishes have received young Christians from other parts of the world. Erick and Elisante, two young men from Tanzania, lived and worked for three months in some parishes in Southern Sweden. Asked what had surprised them most in Sweden, Elisante said, "You don't see one another, and you do not greet one another," and Erick said, "Your worship comes to an end so quickly, and then you just go home."

They remind me of how I myself have experienced the social life in other countries. In the United States, it often happened that a complete stranger made my day a little happier, a little brighter by a kind word at a quick meeting, or in South Sudan, everyone saw and touched everyone else outside the church. Material wealth and social affluence do not necessarily walk hand in hand. But they do not necessarily have to be each other's opposites, either. Why did Erick and Elisante nevertheless find social life in Sweden poorer than at home in Tanzania?

I am convinced that Jante is a culprit in the Swedish drama. There are textbooks in Swedish for immigrants that teach Jante as though it was part of the UN charter, as the journalist and author Maciej Zaremba noted in a series of articles titled *Waiting for Sweden*. If anyone commends you for a brilliant achievement, you should preferably answer, according to this textbook, "Well, it was so-so." It is OK to talk about the weather during the coffee break, but beware of addressing anyone directly, and beware of difficult or controversial issues. Don't get too deep!

Such advice articulates the anxiety about touching and being touched. But in the world of Jante it is, deceitfully enough, called respect for the privacy of other people. Starting a discussion about God at the coffee table cannot be recommended. And if you want to point out some weakness or offer some criticism, Zaremba notes, the textbook suggests the following phrase: "Sometimes I might feel a little bit that you need to practice reading a bit more."

Do we have worse preconditions for social life in Sweden than elsewhere? I do not want to believe that. But I am fairly sure that our fear of coming too close plays many tricks with us. I hate Jante: inwardly it wants to make mincemeat of our self-confidence, and outwardly it makes us scared of coming too close.

How many opportunities to greet a fellow human being with a little smile are missed every day? There are probably thousands of people even today who sit next to one another on buses, trains, airplanes—so close that their upper arms brush against each other, and their elbows collide when they open a newspaper or scroll down their iPads. Many of them will sit down and get up again as if the body next to them was air—even though it belongs to a human being who, according to the Christian faith, is created in the image of God. No greeting, no look, no smile.

It is probably an impossible research project, but I sometimes wonder how much the use of antidepressive drugs would decrease if we saw and greeted one another—even in passing?

Caricatures of Muhammad, Roundabout Dogs, and a Donkey

At about the same time that Denmark had its Muhammad caricatures (2005), Sweden received its roundabout dogs. The caricatures have turned out to have greater longevity than the roundabout dogs. The story of the latter does, however, have attractive features. The roundabout-dog movement started with someone or some group protesting through playful creativity against the vandalism of a work of art. This creative imagination proved contagious and soon became a form of art—a street-art movement that erected dogs in roundabout after roundabout. The "classic" roundabout dog, it is claimed, does not have a pedigree and is not very neat. It is a cross-breed—a street crossing,

GOD IS GREATER

so to speak. It is a protest against the perfect and well-kept roundabout, which, by its empty space in the middle, avoids difficult meetings with crossing traffic. The roundabout dog is a cross-breed in the crossing. At its most successful, it unites joyful zest with a sense of humor, creativity, and protest.

I am attracted by the thought of questioning the roundabouts that we build into our lives, because sometimes we are far too good at constructing roundabouts in order to avoid entangled encounters. The price for not having to tussle with the oncoming person is an empty space at the center! Life is, however, not meant to be organized around an empty space. The intention is that we should meet, learn from one another, and deal with uncomfortable aspects. There should not be an empty space at the center of life. Instead, that is where different streams should meet. This is where we find some of the mystery of vitality and sociability.

How then does Lars Vilks's "Muhammad as a roundabout dog" fit into all this? *(Translator's note: Swedish cartoonist Lars Vilks was invited to participate in a 2007 art exhibition on the theme "The Dog in Art." Vilks submitted three pen-and-ink drawings depicting Muhammad as a "roundabout dog." Vilks's original intention was to "examine the political correctness within the boundaries of the art community.")* In recent years Vilks has participated in various contexts that have been xenophobic and Islamophobic, and he has also become the target of various attempted murders with Islamist overtones, one of which cost two people their lives. Quite regardless of the suitability or unsuitability of the prank of caricaturing Muhammad, the intense debate and the events that followed reveal that one of the most cherished roundabouts in Sweden is a bluff. I refer to the view that religion only belongs to the private sphere and that the center of society constitutes a space that can be free of all religion. The debate has shown that it is rather the opposite. Religion is already there, in the midst of the roundabout, in the midst of the crossing. It relates to all the dimensions of life, the private as well as the political. It must be included in public conversation. Such conversation does not in any way jeopardize democracy. That is, however, what the opposite does, the deportation of religion from the social to the strictly private sphere.

Lars Vilks's drawing of Muhammad as a roundabout dog is not as original as he might have imagined. Already in the third century, a graffitist in Rome drew a picture of the crucified Jesus as a donkey. The picture was equipped with the mocking text "Alexamenos worships his God." A ridiculous God, and an even more ridiculous Alexamenos, who adores a crucified donkey-Christ.

Mobbing and mockery are not the invention of the internet age. They are probably as old as humanity itself. There are scholars who believe that gossip is the cradle of the development of language and of culture. According to that theory, people's needs and tendencies to gossip have speeded up language and have thus lifted social life and the development of culture to new levels. Even though this is only one theory among others, it does put a finger on something fundamental: all contacts, relationships, and institutions have a part in the doubleness that bad intentions can lead to something good, and good intentions can lead to evil.

In spite of his evil intentions, the graffitist in Rome expressed something at the core of Christianity. Ever since Jesus chose to ride into Jerusalem on a donkey on Palm Sunday, we can never get rid of the donkey. Once upon a time the donkey was considered to be a royal animal, but after that it has usually appeared as a symbol for stupidity and rebellion against Roman occupation. Many people thought it was foolish of Jesus not to attempt to assume political power and rebel against

Roman occupation. But in the end, Christianity lives as a result of the fact that he did not do that—and that he identified himself with that stubborn beast of burden instead, with the loads and burdens of the world and of people. He himself became the beast of burden; he carries everything.

The mocking graffitist did something that he was not himself aware of—he painted good theology. In a way he illustrated Paul's words in 1 Corinthians: a crucified Christ is a stumbling block for some, foolishness to others, but for those who believe Christ is the power and wisdom of God (1 Cor 1:23).

The graffiti was good theology. But even good theology can be used destructively—in this case in order to destroy the good reputation of Alexamenos. We do not know what became of him, if he still had any friends after this graffiti, or how his congregation supported him. Maybe he became isolated, even from his own people—you never know, there is probably something wrong with him when things have gone so far. No smoke without a fire! Rumors and opinions begin to live their own life, in the Roman forum as well as on Facebook and Twitter. Evil rumors and unfounded opinions are fertilized by thoughtlessness, laissez-faire, yes-men and -women, and by the far-too-wide-spread view that it is bad manners to become involved. And our need to appoint scapegoats adds to it all.

The Jerusalem that Jesus rode into was a cauldron of rumors and unfounded opinions. There was no clarity about right and wrong, truth and lies. Jesus rode straight into this doubleness. One day jubilant "Hosanna" cries greeted him, the next the cries of "Crucify him." On the one hand loud shouts of joy, on the other reprimands: tell them to shut up! In that doubleness Jesus took up his position: "I tell you, if these were silent, the stones would cry out!" (Luke 19:40). Neutrality is double faced. Not to get involved, to let be, *can* be a virtue, but it is often only a bad cover-up of a deep social poverty. It is part of the mission of the church to counteract such poverty. To live in critical solidarity with society is a way to express love.

Contradiction or Agreement? The Same-Sex-Marriage Issue as an Example

The question of social responsibility in the church can easily become controversial, both from an external and an internal perspective. Sometimes the church's right to "become involved" is questioned from without. From within, various positions are discussed. Does the social responsibility of the church primarily mean to be against and to resist social changes that question ingrained traditions? Or is it primarily a matter of being "in agreement" and of finding biblical and theological motivations for change? Or is it primarily about being prophetic—to question and to point to alternatives?

Sometimes it is right to be against, because we know that a different world is possible. It is an expression of the message and prophetic role of the church. The charge to protect the vulnerable cannot be compromised away. Sometimes it is right to reevaluate the church's own tradition because there are elements that have been long hidden or forgotten and that might become important in the present era. The choice between the alternatives is not always an easy one. What for some people appears to be new thinking in the spirit of the gospel might seem like the church's lack of contours to others. What some people see as authoritarian traditionalism can for others be faithfulness to Christ.

In the discussions on gender-neutral marriages, these two positions were contrasted against one another. *(Translator's note: In May 2009 the Swedish Parliament took the decision to allow marriage between same-sex couples. Later that year the Church of Sweden, as one of the faith denominations that holds the right to officiate at marriage ceremonies in Sweden, considered the question of whether ceremonies of marriage in Church of Sweden churches should be available also for same-sex couples. The General Synod voted yes.)* About the 2009 decision by the Church of Sweden General Synod, some said: "Yes-saying; the church falls flat in the face of the powers of state, with no theological arguments." Others said: "A good consequence of the commandment to love; an expression of theological analysis and the will of the church to support couples in their strivings to live in responsible, life-long relationships of love."

Without going into details about how the arguments ran, I would like to mention in short some of the reasons that I have found to be the most important ones in the discussion in favor of marriage for same-sex couples. Taken altogether, they provide an example of how it is possible to formulate a church position in a situation where church and society have a constructive and mutually critical relationship to one another. In this case the arguments were founded on six key concepts: protection, sacrament, theology of creation, interpretation of Scripture, contemporary knowledge, and synergy.

In the beginning, the discussions focused on the protective function of marriage, which is that marriage gives the couple the protection of society and also contributes to protection for the individual by providing, among other things, a framework for sexuality. Life in faith in the family, and as a family in society and in the world, belong together. There is therefore a point in the fact that it is the state that provides protection for the marriage. It would, however, be a logically wrong conclusion to believe that this protection would be devalued if more people are allowed to receive it.

Marriage has no once-for-all given format. Throughout history, views and rituals around marriage and the family have varied quite considerably. The church speaks of marriage as a gift of God. It is instituted for the sake of maintaining society and as a help and joy for people and for their deeper solidarity. In the Lutheran tradition, marriage is not a sacrament but an institution in society, but even as a social institution it is an aspect of God's care for all people.

Sexual reproduction is part of a pattern in creation, and creation is still in progress. It is not possible to derive any once-and-for-all social orders from an order of creation. That particular way to pursue a theology of creation ended up with a bad reputation when it was used in support of the Nazi ideology during the Third Reich. On the contrary, it is good theology, and entirely in accordance with the spirit of the Bible, to complement the theology of creation with a perspective of justice.

Ethical positions are primarily motivated by the needs of others on the basis of the love commandment rather than from isolated biblical passages. And besides, the passages of Scripture that deal with homosexuality are extremely few and difficult to interpret in their contexts. Justice and poverty are far more frequent themes in the Bible. The New Testament should be interpreted from its central tenet—liberation in Christ to a life of faith and trust, in just, loving, and faithful relationships.

Moreover, theological positions are founded, not only on the Bible, but also on several other sources: tradition, experience, and on contemporary knowledge of relevant subjects. Questions about homosexuality and married life should be treated in the light of the best theological knowledge available to our time in conjunction with the best available knowledge about sexuality, reproduction, and gender identity.

The church's relationship to the state has changed, and nowadays the church goes its own way. That way might, however, very well coincide with that of society without the church therefore abandoning its prophetic role. The gradual changes we have seen in the church since the 1970s on the issue of homosexuality can be understood from that perspective: it is not about a secularized world forcing itself on the church but a mutual impact and a repercussion of Christian secularized values on the church and on theology. The fact that the gospel of Jesus Christ has been preached in Sweden for a thousand years has reasonably influenced the values that we today perceive as secularized. Here is a synergy effect: it might very well be the case that when society confronts the church with critical questions, the church is challenged by the fruits of its own proclamation of the gospel.

Discussions of this kind have been going on in the church from the very beginning. One of the earliest known examples is the debate about circumcision (Acts 15:1–35). Would Christian boys and men of non-Jewish origin need to be circumcised? In that case the liberty line won the victory over the old divinely sanctioned command, in spite of the fact that Jesus himself initially seems to have seen his mission only in relation to his own people, that is, to the people of the circumcision. According to Acts, there was a green light to abstain from circumcision. The prohibition to eat meat that had been used at sacrifices should, however, be strictly kept—a prohibition that Paul later questioned in 1 Corinthians, where he set the love of God and neighbor against knowledge of the applicable regulations. We all know the rules, he said. Yet, "knowledge puffs up, but love builds up" (1 Cor 8:1).

The debate about slavery is yet another example of how people have struggled with an issue on which both sides were convinced that they had found support in the Bible. It provides instructions to slaves, and God is even compared to a slave owner. Yet, even in this case, the liberty and justice line won the victory, albeit far too late.

How well a church can live with different views within itself and in relation to other churches often depends on how well its sense of proportions is functioning. Both theologically and socially, the example of homosexuality has a limited scope. A look in the *Poverty and Justice Bible* is thought provoking. This is an edition of the Bible in which all passages about poverty and justice are highlighted. Such markings appear on almost every page. A corresponding *Sex and Marriage Bible* would have remarkably few markings. Even from a social perspective, homosexual forms of living together affect the view of the family far less than some other social changes might do. According to one newspaper article, more than half of the women inseminated in a Copenhagen clinic in 2008 were single. It is probable that the childhood and life of more young people will be affected by this fact than by growing up with parents of the same gender.

Children, Prayer, and the Right of Access to Stories

Sweden has signed the UN Convention on the Rights of the Child. Its twenty-seventh article lays down the right for every child to have the standard of living that is required for its physical, mental, spiritual, moral, and social development. In Sweden it is considered a societal issue to satisfy these rights—at least with regard to medical care and education. No politician would even remotely suggest that this is a purely private matter. We rightly take it for granted that it is a concern of society as a whole to ensure that the children can have what they need for their physical, psychological, and social needs. With regard to their spiritual, and to some extent also to their moral, developments, views are however not equally clear and self-evident. It is often claimed that religious issues in particular belong to the private sphere only.

It was like that already in the 1980s when I, as a young priest, visited nursery schools within the parish to ask if they might put up a poster to give information to the parents about what opportunities for Sunday school were available for their children. Quite often it was cold-shouldered. No, here we must be neutral. The fact that the majority of the children had actually been baptized and it could therefore be seen as a democratic right for the parents to learn what opportunities for spiritual development were available for them to choose from did not change the situation.

Even to this day passionate letters are written arguing that children should not be exposed to religion, preferably with these arguments: first, children cannot defend themselves against indoctrination, and second, children cannot assimilate religion—to do that, the abstract and critical ability of an adult is required.

Let us take a closer look at these arguments. Children cannot defend themselves against indoctrination. That is true. But by what right do we permit children to be exposed to advertisements? On what basis do we conclude that spending time at a shopping center is less indoctrinating than spending time in a church building? Indoctrination in the sense that an influence on the children takes place without giving them the opportunity to proffer criticism or any discussion of the underlying ideology takes place all the time, whether we like it or not. That is part of the intellectual, emotional, and social development of the child. A world free from ideology would be a sterile world. We need ideologies in the sense of well-thought-out, coherent ideas.

At the same time we need a continuously ongoing ideology critique. There are no sharp borderlines between indoctrinating, giving information, teaching, and nurturing. Nor is there any clear border between an indoctrinating world and a world that is free from all indoctrination. There is however a difference between positive influence and harmful influence. That dividing line does not go between shopping malls, on the one hand, and the church, the mosque, the synagogue, or the temple on the other hand; it might go straight through them all. In both spheres there are opportunities for good as well as for negative influence. There is absolutely nothing to say that a visit to a mall necessarily makes the child a good citizen in society, and that a visit to the church will foist strange ideas about life and death on the child. In fact it might be the very opposite.

Harmful influence is not prevented by making a certain area invisible or suspected and taking a fairly uncritical view of another one. What is needed instead is a constructively critical view in all areas. Spiritual nurturing can go just as astray as intellectual, emotional, and social nurture. It is precisely for that reason that the educational methods in the spiritual area must be used and scrutinized with the same care as in other areas.

Then to the second argument: that children cannot assimilate religion and therefore it is best to keep them in some religious quarantine until they are sufficiently grown up. What is behind such a statement? Is it the view that religion cannot be handled without exercising some kind of violence? Let us for a moment draw a parallel with love. Children can be badly treated, abused, and deeply harmed by perverted love. But nobody would suggest that because of that, children should be kept in a love quarantine until they are sufficiently grown up and able to speak their mind and choose what they want. Nobody would propose a prohibition to touch a child unless the child actively wants it even though, if consequently practiced, this would be the most effective protection against the abuse of children. The price for such protection would of course be death for the child that was to be protected. We know by solid experience that children who do not receive loving touches do not develop normally. In the worst cases, they die.

Hardly any parent would, thank goodness, ask anxiously, Is it right for me to give my child a hug before he or she can decide for him- or herself? However, almost every priest or pastor will at some time or other have met new parents who are struggling with the question whether it is right to let their child be baptized. Is it not more right to wait until he or she can decide for him- or herself? There are thousands of choices that parents must make just because it is not possible to wait until the child can decide for him- or herself. In many of these choices, there is at the time of decision no guarantee whatsoever that, at the end of the day, this choice will turn out to have been the right one. How do parents choose in those circumstances? As a rule, parents choose on the basis of wanting to give their child the best possible presuppositions for its future life. It is about handing on what the parents themselves see as right, good, true, and beautiful. If baptism is part of that, why not give the child access to it? If loving touching is so important, why exclude the touch of divine love, which baptism is?

I would wish that more parents felt free to answer an obvious yes to the question, Is it right to teach my child to pray before he or she comes to think to ask about it? Given that, in many respects, humanity is the most social of all the species that we know about, and that the enormous hunger that human beings have for relationships reaches beyond all the boundaries of their own existence, it seems to be almost a natural need to learn the skill to pray. In other words, to teach children to pray is to open a form of communication for them, for which people in every time and age have felt a strong need. People pray even in one of the most secularized countries in the world—the many thousands of prayers that people have uploaded on the Church of Sweden prayer web testify to that.

Evidence-based experience can be gained in the laboratories of science by testing hypotheses in experiments that can be repeated. But that is not the only place where it can be gained. It is gained to a large extent by living life itself. Prayer can be seen as one of the most well-founded experiences of humanity. It is an ancient form of communication, almost universal, that is even used by people who do not believe in God.

Prayer marks the breath of life of the Christian church. The songs of faith and the language of prayer brood over an enormous treasure of life experience and faith experience. That will be confirmed if you browse through the hymn and prayer books that form such an important part of the Christian tradition.

Prayer unites deeply personal experience with the universally human experience. I can recognize myself and at the same time feel carried by a "we." I can feel that it is not I who carry the prayer but the prayer that carries me. I might also encounter something that seems strange to my life and my environment but that is or has been strongly present to people in other places and ages. This is reflected in the tradition of the Divine Office, which has been there throughout the entire history of the church. The offices, which are built up on the psalms in the Bible, are a tradition of prayer that has survived throughout the centuries, both as common and as private prayer. The psalms of the Bible, with their colorful mix of devotion and cheekiness, wrath and wisdom, anxiety and security, lamentation and praise show that prayer is about being able to communicate "how things really are."

We know by experience that children are very capable of assimilating and reasoning about spiritual matters—often with insights that we adults have forgotten but do well to be reminded of. What children and youth need is not a spiritual quarantine until they are able to think in abstract terms but tools for spiritual development. That is primarily the responsibility of the parents and the communities of faith. It is an urgent responsibility because critical skills are needed in the spiritual area as well. And those are never acquired without knowledge and practice.

Student chaplains are worried about increasing mental health issues among young people. Prayer and faith do not vaccinate against psychological problems, but faith and prayer are certainly an asset—both in biting wind and when life is at its most beautiful. Some of the problems that young adults are struggling with today are linked to a lack of spiritual development and spiritual resistance as well as a lack of experience of sustaining and nourishing communities.

Human growth and maturity are dependent on material standards and intellectual work. But neither the wallet nor reason can suffice all the way. The generosity of heart and of emotions is built on more than that. That is the insight I discern beyond the breadth of article 27 of the Convention of the Rights of the Child about the physical, mental, spiritual, moral, and social development of the child.

The view that children are not able to assimilate religion militates against Christian tradition and experience. The message of Jesus is clear: children are the greatest in the kingdom of heaven (Matt 18:1–5); children are receptive to the reign of God in a way that adults need to learn (Mark 10:13–16). That was a radical point in the society at that time. And this point has had an echo in the Church of Sweden Introduction to the Church Order (regulations about the organization and work of the church). There it says: "In the Christian faith, children hold a unique position and they should receive particular attention in the work of the Church of Sweden."

The child's right to spiritual development includes—besides access to the holy rooms, rites, customs, and practices of their own faith tradition—also access to its treasures of narratives. It is remarkable that our time in particular questions the common right of everyone to the great stories. When nursery-school children's right to see a "live" nativity play is questioned, the common rights of everyone to the Christmas story are called into question. But the great stories are for everyone; their place is not in the private, closed-off room. The really great narratives want to be told over and over again. When the shepherds had made their visit to the manger on Christmas night, the great storytelling starts: "they made known what had been told them about this child, and all who heard it were amazed" (Luke 2:17–18).

The Christmas gospel is a good example of a story that is common property in the best sense of the word. It is about "great joy *for all the people*" (Luke 2:10, emphasis added) that has had an effect in many popular practices around the celebrations of Christmas. Such a story is not the exclusive property of any particular group. The stories in the Hebrew Bible about exodus, jealousy, oppression, and liberation, of Job's struggles as well as the parables of Jesus and the stories about his life, death, and resurrection can be viewed in the same way. These stories struggle with universal human issues, and they offer so many openings for interpretation and have so many emotional resonances that everyone might be touched somewhere. Here is something that is right! Here are dreams, visions, and ideas that touch us.

I am convinced that it is worth protecting everyone's rights to access to the great stories if for no other reason than to show that there are several other alternatives than the choice between authoritarian religious indoctrination on the one hand, and the nurturing of children into religious illiterates on the other.

It matters what religious traditions are handed on to children in a society. As an example, I quote from the ethicist Emilie M. Townes (b. 1955), who is one of the few black women to hold a prominent position in the American academic world.

> This is where the church of my youth was so important, for it continually reinforced the message that I was receiving from my parents, my grandmother, and the adults in my neighborhood and school: you are a child of God, God loves you, God will protect you, and you are a child of worth who can do anything you set your mind to. In short, I was surrounded with loving and caring people; they were far from perfect, but they were relentless in passing along their care, and they taught that we must do likewise with others—that this was fundamental to being a Christian . . . It was in this space that I learned that the church could and should combine a lively and soul-deep spirituality with a vital and active social witness.

Experiences of holiness are a constant subtext in the history of humankind. They have followed human beings continually throughout our evolution. The thought that we, particularly in our day and age, should have broken with that is quite improbable. There have probably never been any absolutely unambiguous boundaries between the religious and the non-religious, or between the cultural and the religious spheres. There is instead an overlap, which certainly has its risks, but which throughout the ages has caused much creative energy, exciting debates, and dynamic societal development to emerge.

Sect Warnings and Confessional Neutrality

A democratic state should be secular. That does not, however, mean that society must also be secular. As long as there are people who belong to religious traditions, a society is not secular. Freedom of religion, which implies freedom both for and from religion, is important for the social life in a secular, democratic state. It is the task of the state to create frameworks that enable good developments in society. This task may appear as more demanding the more pluralism there is in society. At the same time, plurality can provide fertile soil for creativity.

Sweden has a preference for neutrality. Neutrality has kept us safe from two world wars during the twentieth century and from many other troubles, Swedes tend to say. This makes it easy to claim neutrality as a winning concept even with regard to order in a multicultural society. It could be interpreted as if democracy, openness, freedom, and plurality are dependent on a sharp dividing line between the secular, which we call neutral, and the religious, which some people call superstitious and others a special interest and a private matter. Such a dividing line has two consequences. First, faith becomes a problem in society rather than an asset. Faith will be tolerated as long as it does not make itself felt—the less it is noticed, the better. Second, democracy will be exalted to something that seems to be free from all the values of any conception of life, and the norm that is expected to create unity in society. The ideal citizen is then a person who stands above all religion. Democracy becomes the story in which all hopes are united in a way that makes religious faith appear as primarily a factor of disturbance.

This is a very oversimplified picture. Democracy does not exist anywhere as a chemically pure substance in a vacuum, and it is never free from the threat and the risk of failure. The free, secular state is dependent on presuppositions that it cannot guarantee by itself. It is not necessary to be a believer yourself; it is enough to be like the "religiously unmusical" but wise philosopher Jürgen Habermas (b. 1929), who has understood how naive it is to imagine that secular democracy is entirely self-sufficient. Democracy is neither self-sustaining nor immune. It is precisely for that reason that it is so important that all good forces should take care to protect its survival. In order to keep healthy and vital, democracy is dependent on being nurtured by values. Therefore it must constantly be charged with energy from values that are born of the encounter with humanity's major traditions of ideas. Open, critical, and constructive listening is as important for democracy as the free press is. A secular democracy that closes its ears to others is just as problematic as a religious dogmatism that does the same thing. It can therefore never be the case that believers must one-sidedly adapt to a secular norm. In a good society, there must be mutual learning.

Sometimes I wonder when people stopped saying, "He is a good guy; he is a believer" and started implying instead, "He is a good guy *although* he is a believer." When did it come about that people began to feel that their faith ends up being a liability rather than an asset when they are judged? When did all religion receive the stamp of a sect? And why? It would be a gigantic waste of hope and faith to assume that believers are by definition a problem in a modern democracy, and that they are unsuited to exercising important social functions if they do not hide their faith.

In a municipality in Skåne (Scania), the Church of Sweden and a care trust joined forces in order to start a hospice. The project was questioned by politicians because the intention was that its work would rest on a Christian basis. Then not everybody can be admitted, the critics thought. A "Christian basis" was perceived as equal to being exclusive. This criticism is remarkable. It is a pillar of the Christian faith to love one's neighbor, even one's enemy, regardless of their background. The parable of the good Samaritan (Luke 10:30–37) is fundamental to Christian ethics, which has always been a strong driving force for providing care, and in the Bible, the stories about Jesus's encounters with those who are different and alien are among the most persuasive. Of course hospice work on a Christian basis is open to everyone—otherwise it would not rest on a Christian foundation. And of course a Christian view of life can be discussed and talked about in universal human words—otherwise it would not be credible.

The discussion about the hospice is worrying if it

stands for a trend—namely for the trend to issue a sect warning as soon as there is talk of religion. Where that happens, intelligent conversation will be hindered, and misunderstandings will flourish. Something strange has happened if the Christian message and Christian practice can be considered as offensive in principle and should therefore preferably be deported to a ghetto. One might wonder how anyone can feel offended by values that stand for love of neighbor! How can one feel offended by hearing that even those who fail are accepted? (And those who fail are not always "the others"!)

Can anyone be offended because someone wishes you God's peace or because someone says, "I pray for you"? Maybe. When Jesus sent his friends out on a mission, he taught them to greet people with a greeting of peace. And if people did not want to receive the peace, the friends should be sure that the peace would return to themselves. And in that case, they should just shake the dust off their feet and go on elsewhere (Luke 10:5–11).

Is there something dangerous about a Christianity that aims to foster free, loving people who will seek the best for this world? Is there something dangerous with people who seek to express joy over their belonging to God, to one another, and to the whole creation together with all other people of good will? People who strive for love, joy, peace, patience, kindness, generosity, faithfulness, gentleness, and self-control (the fruits of the Spirit according to Gal 5:22)? People who seek to protect human dignity, the weak, the children—and article 27 of the Convention on the Rights of the Child as a whole?

Offense against human beings is something serious. Such things must not be played down. And for that reason, the term must not be misused either. And therefore I continue to wonder: can anyone be offended by hearing, "You are inviolable in your human dignity because I believe that you are loved by God and created for living in community"? Can one really be offended by being told that one is inviolable?

We live in a world in which human dignity is violated daily in many ways. People are deprived of their right to food, clothes, and a home to live in. They are deprived of education, medical care, and the right to development. Against this background, some so-called offenses appear at best as a luxury problem.

Schools may be seen as a test case for the borderline between the secular state and non-secular society. There is, on the one hand, good and respectful collaboration between church and school, and sometimes even between mosque and school. There are many teachers who gratefully receive a visit by a parish worker, a deacon, or a priest in their class—because they have seen competence that is good for the class, for the pupils, for the teacher, and for the school. In situations of crisis, collaboration with the church is usually taken for granted, in society at large as in the school. On the other hand, the school is not permitted to engage in confessional education. This is absolutely right—but it does not mean that the school automatically stands above all kinds of confessions. Adherence to no creed whatsoever is not an easy requirement to fulfill. If one confession is shown the door with great hullabaloo, there is always the risk that another, less-tested one might slink in through the back door. It is therefore no solution to ignore religious or political confessions or to make them invisible.

The question is whether we need to turn the perspective around and consider confessions as opportunities rather than problems. True professionalism is not built on leaving all creeds behind. The ideal of the room without adherence to any confession is a chimera. Maybe it is rather the case that true professionalism also requires deliberate confessionalism—confessionality that is aware of its strength and its limits. What is actually needed all the time with regard to confessionality is critical attention in relation to the current context.

Non-confessional teaching is not the same as denying a cultural heritage. European culture is deeply marked by the great Christian stories. Without them it is impossible to understand Händel's "Messiah," Ingmar Bergman's films, Elisabeth Ohlson-Wallin's photo exhibitions, many modern novels, or the singularly greatest coherent cultural heritage of Sweden, the church buildings.

To be a non-confessionalist is not as easy as dismissing religion as faith in something supernatural—and to propagate science instead as a guarantor of neutrality. No area of knowledge is entirely separated from values that spring from a conception of life. As I will go on to discuss (see chaps. 2–3), Christian faith is not the same as faith in something supernatural. One of the most important stories of Christianity—the Christmas gospel—questions precisely the division into natural and supernatural. The story is about the presence of God in the natural sphere. That sets a fundamental tone for a Christian view of life and for the life and work of the church in the world.

In spite of the absence of sharp dividing lines, it is still possible to distinguish between the handing down of tradition and indoctrination. The handing on of traditions obviously includes religious traditions—and that is much needed. Indoctrination in the sense that a certain teaching is proclaimed as the only right one is reprehensible. A well-performed end-of-term service in church, for example, is not indoctrination, but it furthers familiarity with a cultural and religious heritage. Only people who are familiar with cultural and religious concepts can develop a mature and critical attitude toward them.

We see a world today in which the importance of religion is increasing, for better or worse. Fundamentalism is a danger, regardless of where it stems from. Good knowledge of religious and existential issues is an advantage in a democratic society. If we nurture our children to become religiously illiterate, they will be very badly equipped as citizens in today's and tomorrow's world. They will be easy prey for fundamentalist tendencies, and they will find it more difficult to orientate in the world of conceptions of life. Islamist leaders are probably well aware why they recommend that suicide bombers should be recruited among secular men. Religiously illiterate people or recent converts will fall more easily for fanatic propaganda than people who are so rooted in their faith tradition that they can relate to it critically and self-critically.

It is sometimes said that we must keep the public arena free of religion for the sake of our immigrants, and then the reference is usually to Muslims. Muslims are no more a homogeneous group than any others. There are major differences among and between groups of immigrants. Church workers sometimes speak of meetings with Muslims who prefer a spiritual environment rather than a purely secular one. That means that they would rather have a Christian environment than one that bans religious issues and reduces them to a private matter.

God's House: Ecumenism in Our Day and Age

While Sibiu in Romania was the European cultural capital in 2007, the city also hosted the Third General Assembly of the Ecumenical European Church Conference (CEC). In Sibiu there were 2,500 delegates from European Christian churches gathered for lectures, hearings, consultation, and worship.

I was not a member of the official delegation, but

I had the benefit of being present for the conclusion of this major ecumenical meeting. It was wonderful to hear the languages mix, to enter into spontaneous conversations with unknown women and men because you are curious of one another. The city was teeming with Christians of various shades—people in civilian dress, clerical collars, and monks' and nuns' habits of various kinds, and not least the Orthodox dignitaries in their long black coats and impressive headgear. My episcopal shirt blended well into the picture, even though it caused some curiosity that it was a woman wearing it. It opened doors that are officially closed. When Roman Catholic and Orthodox nuns rejoice at the sight of this particular episcopal shirt, when an Orthodox priest comes up to shake hands, when a Roman Catholic archbishop starts a collegial conversation—then there is hope and joy in ecumenism. Grassroots ecumenism is flourishing, even among ordained ministers.

I heard someone in Sibiu say: "I have realized here that the European idea is carried by and lives in the Christian churches." And it is important that we show that European collaboration is not only about capital, consumption, and goods but also about spiritual community. More than ten years later, when European collaboration has been severely tested by financial crises, Brexit, and a demanding number of refugees, these words appear as even more relevant and urgent.

Ecumenism is the churches' attempt to live out the belief that God is greater—greater than their own denomination as well. It is stimulating indeed to participate in conversations across boundaries—whether it is across linguistic, cultural, or denominational boundaries. After the Second World War, ecumenism went through an enthusiastic stage. In a Europe devastated by bombings, the churches united in a common affirmation: "Never again!" Toward the end of the twentieth century, the ecumenical embers cooled somewhat. Some things even moved backward.

The optimists see this as a sign that the dialogue has entered a more mature stage. Others believe that the end of the road has been reached. Yet others question the "old boys' ecumenism," that is, the long series of meetings and conversations between theologians and church leaders about what we are agreed on and on what theological issues we differ. Instead, grassroots ecumenism is recommended, that is, common action instead of (or maybe as a necessary complement to) conversations and agreements. As archbishop, I certainly do not think that doctrinal conversations are unimportant, but my heart also beats strongly for the "ecumenism of the feet." If this is carried out well, I believe it can liberate the "ecumenism of the head" where that might have become stuck.

In the light of the most urgent challenges that humanity is facing, traditional forms of ecumenism might be a bit like an afternoon tea party while the house is on fire. Maybe we sometimes need to leave the doctrinal issues aside for a while and focus instead on the common task, thus moving our powers from dialogue to dia-praxis. If the author of Ephesians is right, we can afford to do that: "There is . . . one God and Father of all, who is above all and through all and in all" (Eph 4:4–6)—also above our doctrinal differences. If God works through all and is in all, as Ephesians also says, we can afford to be generous and courageous: generous in our choice of conversation partners and courageous in our attempts to give words and body to the gospel.

There is always a risk that ecumenism is used as a weapon in our internal church discussions. That happened in the discussions about the ordination of women to the priesthood, and it is also happening with regard to issues of sexual ethics. Where is the proper balance between daring to go ahead and showing respect for the situation of other churches, which might demand quite different priorities? Even ecumenical arguments must be seen in their respective contexts. That the Church of England, for example, gave priority to the unity of the Anglican Communion rather than engaging in the struggle with issues of sexual ethics has to do with the aftermaths of colonialism. In order to understand the strong opposition to homosexuality in the African churches while polygamy is accepted in certain contexts, it is necessary to be aware of the cultural, religious, and postcolonial situation. Arguments that are taken out of their contexts are suitable for stating incompatibility or to demonstrate irreconcilability. Arguments that are understood in relation to their context make it possible, on the other hand, to continue the conversation—by accepting the differences of the positions and striving for reconciled diversity or common action (diapraxis). This insight makes a difference. In spite of differences in our views of homosexuality and same-gender relationships, bishops from the Church of Sweden and from Tanzania were able to express their will together to "share and respect theology shaped by our traditions and the contexts in which we live" at a joint bishops' meeting in 2015.

Today the joint Christian work in the world is to a great extent about together finding the prophetic voice that can awaken people's desire to change their lifestyle for the sake of justice, peace, and creation. Christian faith has something to offer when gloomy prognoses create anxiety. We believe in a living Christ who comes to meet us in every time, not in a long-dead human being. Our joy in Christ and our joy in creation are driving forces that the world needs.

Interfaith Dialogue Is an Awakening

During the autumn of 2007, 138 Muslim scholars from different countries wrote an open letter to the pope and other Christian leaders. In that letter they pointed, in a clear and obvious manner, to a common foundation for Christians and Muslims, namely to the commandment to love God and neighbor. The Muslim leaders also noted that Christians and Muslims together make up the majority of the population of the world. From that they drew the reasonable conclusion that good relationships between Christians and Muslims are absolutely necessary for the peace of the world. And who does not want to work for peace in the world?

In spite of these good intentions, developments have moved in the opposite directions since then. The Arab Spring did not turn into a summer. The war in Syria; the tensions throughout that entire region; the terrible ravages against people and culture for which Daesh (IS) bears responsibility; the persecutions of Christians and other groups; acts of terrorism; the lack of solidarity in Europe with regard to the reception of refugees; the inability of the world community to cut off the supplies of money and arms to terrorist organizations; increasing nationalism, polarization, xenophobia, and Islamophobia—the list of things that endanger welfare and peace, locally, regionally, and globally, could be made long.

In January 2016, the initiative from 2007 was followed up by a conference in Marrakesh in Morocco, which gathered several hundred participants from more than 120 countries: Muslim scholars and intellectuals, and representatives of governments and Muslim international organizations as well as leaders of other religious groups, such as Christians, Jews, and Yazidis. The result was the Marrakesh Declaration on the Rights of Religious Minorities in countries that have a primarily Muslim majority. That declaration affirms that it is unconscionable to use religion for the purpose of aggressing upon the rights of religious minorities in Muslim countries. Citizenship is a key concept. The declaration includes a reminder of the times when various religious groups have lived together in peace and speaks of the necessity to regain the confidence that extremists have destroyed through acts of terrorism and aggression.

The declaration recalls the principles of the 1,400-year-old Charter of Medina from the age of the Prophet Muhammad. There the religious liberty of all inhabitants, regardless of their faith, was guaranteed, and this constitution could be said to deliver a framework for understanding the UN Declaration of Human Rights. It is stressed that the crises that are facing humanity require collaboration between different religious groups. On the basis of the 2007 initiative, the Marrakesh Declaration confirms that such collaboration must be about more than one-sided tolerance and respect. It must include the full protection by the state of the rights and liberties of all religious groups. Representatives of all religions are encouraged to confront every form of narrowmindedness and contempt for others and to show mutual solidarity. The civil societies in Muslim countries are also encouraged to work for a broad movement toward a just treatment of religious minorities.

From a Christian perspective, the implication is that, as a religious minority in a Muslim country, Christians should be fully included in society, enjoy protection from persecution, and have their rights guaranteed by law and in practice. This is expressed in good words, to which reality so far corresponds far too rarely. The Declaration is therefore important, and it needs to be made widely known and spoken of as the exhortation that it actually is. Reality is seldom changed for the better unless a vision is put into words. In the beginning was the Word: that applies not only to creation as such but also to the creation of peace.

World peace hardly comes by itself—it requires an effort by all people of good will. This effort often begins by creating dialogue at the local level. Some rules of thumb are important for a successful conversation: to describe the other so that he or she can recognize him- or herself; not to compare the best in your own tradition with the worst in the other; to know that you can admire something in the other tradition and at the same time love your own.

The history of Europe is marked by wars and conflicts. We Europeans have not always managed to live as good neighbors with those we have perceived as aliens. But we also have examples of how Christians, Jews, and Muslims have lived together with welfare and a flourishing cultural life as a result. Everyone who has visited Granada, Seville, Cordoba, or Toledo cannot have failed to notice the historical testimonies from this period of peaceful conviviality.

Today's reality is not unambiguous. We see successful conversations, good collaboration, and friendship across cultural and religious boundaries. And at the same time we see frightening signs of conflict, alienation, and violence. We have long been worried that Christian minorities in the world have increasingly hard times because they have been seen as representatives of politics and history from which people want to distance themselves. And even worse. During the 2010s, persecution of Christians and other believers increased dramatically, particularly in the Middle East.

I grew up in Germany in a society that had the horrors of Nazism and anti-Semitism in fresh memory. I was brought up to be aware of the wiliness of achieving shifts of values that could become truly catastrophic through sneakingly insidious changes to the language. It happens, for example, by bundling together a large group of people with major internal differences between them, labeling them with an ethnic or religious stamp, and then presenting them as a collective threat.

The fact that our reality rarely agrees with the ideals should not stop us from seeking to win a common ground. That requires mutual learning, conversation, and collaboration around common tasks in society and—not least—true friendship between those who hold key positions within various groups in society.

Societies that manage to take care of differences in a positive way are more creative and stable in the long run than those that set "us" and "them" against one another or pretend that we are all the same.

The commandment to love motivates us to choose the way of creativity. The question we should ask ourselves is not "How can we survive multiculture?" but "How can we survive monoculture?" That is not saying that life in diversity is an easy life. Complexity can imply suffering—that applies to both natural and social processes.

Almost five decades ago a Swedish bishop made the then not entirely uncontroversial statement in his pastoral letter to the Diocese of Lund: "Being turned toward society is not a heresy but an awakening." This statement can be accompanied today by another:

"Interfaith dialogue is not a heresy but an awakening." Maps are being redrawn, and borders change their character. Where simple explanations have played out their role, new conversations become possible, and new identities can emerge. That does not mean any equalization of differences or a life without conflicts. But it does mean great opportunities for development in areas where there is an overlapping consensus. To engage in interfaith dialogue is a rational choice in our time. The international political situation does not make it any easier but all the more urgent. Interreligious dialogue is and remains a necessity for peaceful coexistence.

In the face of the major global challenges of our time, the most difficult hindrances are shortsightedness, narrowmindedness, and nationalism. The national state—the political model according to which every people with their own language in principle have their own state—may have been a useful precondition for developments during the nineteenth century. It has hardly ever been consequently put into practice however, and during the twentieth century it gradually ended up in a crisis. In the twenty-first century, on the one hand, nationalism as a bearing idea seems increasingly controversial, and we seek, with varying success, forms of organization that enable global responsibility. On the other hand, we have seen nationalist movements spreading anew across many countries.

It is plausible that one governing system is not enough, and that there is instead a need for collaboration between different systems of governance. In this collaboration, communities and institutions must aim to assess the threats currently facing the environment and climate and carry out suitable measures against them. There is also a need for greater efforts toward peace, in which systems of governance strive for consistent progress on the issues of poverty, migration, and integration and work to minimize political violence and extremism.

As society becomes increasingly multicultural, religious communities have even greater potential to foster connection and meaning. Many religious communities are multicultural from the beginning, or have at least the theoretical preconditions for being inclusive. The so-called Great Commission (Matt 28:18–20) attracted a bad reputation because, for a while, Christian mission went hand in hand with colonialism. Criticism of oppressive mission activities has sometimes obscured the good aspects of mission. In the wake of this criticism, it was easy to forget that the call to baptism and mission is a call to include others and transcend borders.

Religious communities also have a potential for furthering a culture of social cohesion, which can be an asset for any society. Modern Western societies risk keeling over toward individualism whenever individual rights are stressed at the cost of efforts on behalf of the common good. When consumption and overconsumption become more prominent activities than building for the common good, problems arise.

Facing the greatest challenges of our time requires a sense of social cohesion, which is built up by giving and taking, and by solidarity with the commandment to love. It also requires a readiness to change that touches people's deepest values.

Interfaith meetings are becoming increasingly common, even in church contexts. We have come to a point at which ecumenism (from the Greek *oikoumene*, "the inhabited world") can no longer be limited to the Christian denominations. True ecumenism must reach further than to the different rooms of the Christian mansion. In that spirit, the 2012 Church of Sweden General Synod added the following sentence to the church order: "On the basis of the faith of the church in

God as creating, redeeming and life-giving throughout the world, the wider ecumenical calling means to work for the unity of the church, the community of humanity and the healing of the world, and to seek God's address in the encounter with every person, regardless of their religious tradition." It is good that this is being said at a time when we have learned that a well-functioning dialogue is not the same as agreeing on the lowest common denominator. It is from "our own" that it is possible to build bridges to "the alien" through recognition or through common understanding in sensitivity to the questions, needs, and challenges of the world. Thus we can see the interplay that makes it possible for Christians to be the church in critical solidarity with society and the world.

2

After Secularization: The Time for Simple Explanations Is Past

A recently graduated high school teacher receives a completely new class to teach. It consists of sixteen young people who have recently arrived in Sweden, most of them on their own. Their mother tongues vary from English and Polish to Arabic and Dari.

After a week the teacher takes the students for an outing in Malmö. They need to learn how to read bus timetables and how to borrow books from the library. When they pass a church, some of the young men ask if they are allowed to go in, even though they are Muslims. When the answer is yes, they go in and look around. They discover the stickers with requests for intercessions and ask if they might write some prayers themselves. They do. "We have prayed for Iraq," they tell the teacher a little later.

The young teacher starts thinking. What is actually normal for a human being? To be religious, and to seek to express your spirituality? Or to deny your religiosity and to consider yourself stronger and freer if you do not need any holy space?

Having grown up in a secular environment like Sweden, it is easy to get the impression that it is normal not to be religious. But of the almost 7.5 billion people in the world, there are far more whose daily life includes religious practices than those whose life does not. Seen from a global perspective, it is the Swedish society that is deviant.

So how Christian is Europe, in fact? That question was put to me by an American professor of Jewish studies, and I found it difficult to answer, especially since it was asked in front of an international and multireligious audience. It is obviously impossible to understand the history of Europe if you do not know anything about the Christian faith and the church. Education, medical care, social care, the arts, music, literature, architecture, philosophy, science, politics, wars and conflicts—none of these elements of European history can be understood without a fairly good knowledge of Christianity. Even so, the traditional term "the Christian West" does not seem quite right. Secularization has changed the religious map, not least in Sweden. The fact that the majority of people nevertheless belong to a Christian church makes it all the more fascinating. That was roughly how I tried to answer, until it dawned on me that my Jewish friend actually only wanted to test me. Therefore I eventually returned the question with the words, "You, as a historian, probably know more about this than I do!"

"Of course Europe is Christian," was his answer. "European history and the present cannot be understood without the story of Jesus Christ and the various interpretations that this narrative has been given over the centuries." It all sounded so obvious. And how wholesome it can be to look at one's own identity as mirrored in someone else's view. From a Swedish perspective it is easy to get stuck in an understanding of religious liberty as primarily freedom from religion—and to forget the fact that it is just as much about freedom to have and to practice a religion.

But how Christian is Europe actually—and Sweden?

Christianity has not grown up on European soil. How did it get there? In the book of Acts, we find a description of how the church began in Europe. Historically, we cannot be sure whether this actually was Europe's first encounter with the story of Jesus Christ. Luke does, however, narrate the arrival of Christianity in Europe in a way that is relevant for the self-understanding of the Christian church even today.

> During the night Paul had a vision: there stood a man of Macedonia pleading with him and saying, "Come over to Macedonia and help us." When he had seen the vision, we [Paul, Silas, and Timothy] immediately tried to cross over to Macedonia, being convinced that God had called us to proclaim the good news to them. We set sail from Troas and took a straight course to Samothrace, the following day to Neapolis, and from there to Philippi, which is a leading city of the district of Macedonia and a Roman colony. We remained in this city for some days. On the sabbath day we went outside the gate by the river, where we supposed there was a place of prayer, and we sat down and spoke to the women who had gathered there. A certain woman named Lydia, a worshiper of God, was listening to us; she was from the city of Thyatira and a dealer in purple cloth. The Lord opened her heart to listen eagerly to what was said by Paul. When she and her household were baptized, she urged us, saying "If you have judged me to be faithful to the Lord, come and stay at my home." And she prevailed upon us. (Acts 16:9–15)

GOD IS GREATER

Thus three men took the boat from Troas in Asia Minor across the Aegean Sea. The winds were favorable. It took them only two days to reach the Port of Neapolis, on European soil. And they soon arrived in Philippi, a central town in Macedonia but at that particular time a Roman colony.

It was a strange story that made these three men turn up in Europe. Paul had traveled around in Asia Minor, where he had preached the gospel of Jesus Christ and founded a number of congregations. He was a bit frustrated because it had not been all that easy. His plans for building parishes had failed now and again. Now he was wondering where to turn next. Did God have a plan for this work, or was it time to reconsider? In that conundrum Paul had a dream. He saw a Macedonian man who asked him, "Come across to Macedonia and help us." Paul heard the cry of that man as the call of God and set out for Europe together with his little team.

And that is why Paul, Silas, and Timothy were now walking around Philippi, looking for the man from the dream. However, the dream-man never turned up in reality. Or rather, the dream-man was in fact a woman by the name of Lydia, as it turned out. They met her on the Sabbath. By then they had spent several days trying in vain to make contact in Philippi. Now they decided to go outside the city, to the river, where they supposed there would be a place to pray. They sat down together with some women and ended up in a serious and committed conversation. One of the women was Lydia. According to the book of Acts, she was the first person in Europe to become a Christian.

Who was Lydia? She was an immigrant, and she ran her own business. She originated from the country of Lydia, which is in present-day Turkey, and she worked with importing and selling purple cloth, an attractive consumer good at that time. And she turned out to be a real dream-woman when it came to preaching the gospel of Jesus Christ. The success of the mission in Europe began with telling the story at that place of prayer by the banks of the river. But it does not end there. The circle of storytelling soon transformed into a baptismal procession when Lydia and all her household were baptized. Then the baptismal group soon became a meal fellowship when Paul, Silas, and Timothy were urged to stay with Lydia. Together with her household, they created the first Christian church in Europe, a household church in Philippi.

A goal had been reached, but it had certainly not happened the way that Paul had imagined. Rather than making serious contacts in the synagogue as usual, he had to find a place of prayer outside the city. Rather than meeting at least ten men who celebrated a real service of worship on the Sabbath, he found a group of women in conversation. Rather than the expected dream-man, a woman appeared. Paul also had to break his own principle never to take advantage of the hospitality of new Christians in order not to compromise his missionary charge. The three men had to change their minds, move in with Lydia, and receive bread from her hand because, as the text points out, she did not give in—she "prevailed upon us"!

According to the book of Acts, this was the beginning of Christianity in Europe, in the place that would later on proudly call itself "the Christian West": an apostle who had to rethink, point by point, a woman who did not give up, and who therefore became the leader of the first Christian church on European soil. One of the points of this story is this: whoever wants to work for God does well to be flexible—prepared to be surprised—and open to what is different. It was quite a lot that was demanded from Paul in that respect.

Surprises and openness to what is different are still required today with regard to faith and encounters with religion as a many-faceted phenomenon. For quite a while now we have heard talk of the return of religion or the new visibility of religion.

The time for simple explanations is past. We know today that secularization never became a straightforward development toward the death of faith. And we can see a growing interest in spirituality walking hand in hand with enormous ignorance about the Christian faith. Rite and religion are the in-thing, but church and Christianity are less so, one might say. The Church of Sweden is one of the largest Lutheran churches in the world while Sweden is at the same time considered to be one of the most secularized nations in the world. Since the year 2000, the church has been separated from the state. Sweden is a country whose culture is formed by Christian traditions but at the same time wants to be multicultural, providing space for a multiplicity of denominations and traditions. This is an exciting and demanding challenge!

In 1992 the then-chairman of the EU Commission, Jacques Delors, reminded church leaders of the need to give a soul, spirituality, and meaning to Europe. That, he suggested, should be a priority for the next ten years, since Europe would not come about only through legal statutes or by a certain amount of financial know-how. He recognized a lack of authentic inspiration and vision for the future, for which he thought the churches were partly to blame.

I am not going to consider here whether we have succeeded or failed in the task that Delors envisaged in the early 1990s. But even though Europe's soul is not Christian in any exclusive sense, it is hardly possible to understand it without that which began at the place of prayer outside Philippi. The text about Lydia says something about the way in which the church contributes to the life of the soul of civilization.

A significant point is that Christianity in Europe began with the baptism of an immigrant, a devout woman who ran her own business. This openness to the surprisingly different, and maybe even alien, was a hallmark of the Christian church. It was also the hallmark of Jesus's own attitude—openness not only to money-making tax collectors and other sinners but also to strangers and foreigners, such as the Canaanite woman that he first turned away because he assumed that he had only been sent to the Jews (Matt 15:21–28). Even Jesus could reconsider and think something new—just as God could change plans with regard to the city of Nineveh, which we are told about in the book of Jonah in the Old Testament. Whoever grapples with the promises of God can afford to take on board new insights.

Thus it is a point that we do need others, those who are different and think differently. We need our relationships with other denominations and churches, with our international contacts and our exchanges with women and men of other faiths. Hospitality is a holy duty that unites us Christians with other faith traditions. Lydia's example shows how decisive hospitality can be.

Another point in the story is that the way of the church begins with the word: through conversation, teaching, and fellowship, and in due course baptism and Eucharist. Preaching, baptism, Eucharist, community—that is what constitutes the church. Violence and force do not belong there. There have been times when this has been forgotten. Then the church allied itself to the sword. But the first Christian church on European soil provides the view that faith is born from narrative and conversation, and from attentive listening (Rom 10:17). Lydia was sensitive to the gospel.

It is hard not to be curious about what Paul actually said to Lydia and what made her and her household wanting baptism promptly. Luke does not reveal that in his story. A qualified guess is that he hardly mentioned the adage, "Women should be silent in the churches" (cf. 1 Cor 14:33–34). Probably rather something like what he said with such pregnancy in his letter to the Galatians: "As many of you as were baptized into Christ have clothed yourselves with Christ. There is no longer Jew or Greek, there is no longer slave or free, there is no longer male or female; for all of you are one in Christ Jesus" (Gal 3:27–28).

Lydia is a good model for the Christian life: enterprising, energetic, sensitive, hospitable, and also gifted with perseverance: "And she prevailed upon us." Her argument is "authenticity." If you can find authenticity in me, she argued against Paul and his team, you have no other choice but to share the meal fellowship with me, fully and altogether. Paul saw authenticity in Lydia, and he respected her leadership.

That is how I want to see the presence of the church in today's world: authentic, enterprising, energetic, sensitive, hospitable, and persevering.

Between the Return of Religion and the Crusades of Atheism

Europe's history is a history of linguistic, cultural, and religious plurality. Sometimes we think that multiculturalism is something new, peculiar to our time. But multicultural societies have existed long before us. They have probably always existed, although in different forms. In medieval Spain, Jews, Christians, and Muslims lived together with intense exchanges among one another. Peaceful coexistence and conflicts have succeeded one another; migrations have created conflicts but have also renewed societies.

It was in fact only when I was living outside Europe for some years that I thought I could develop a more nuanced view of the interplay between unity and plurality in religion, culture, and ethnicity. The United States is proud of its diversity. Even so, you can travel from east to west, from north to south in this enormous country without having to change language, without having to know all that many food cultures, media channels, or newspapers. Travel the same time and distance in Europe, and count the languages, menus, TV channels, and major daily papers that you need to relate to during that journey! The difference is significant. In spite of all this, it did happen in the US that I was accused of Eurocentrism—that is, of taking a one-sidedly Eurocentric perspective, as if there was only one such perspective. What is perceived as unity or diversity is very often dependent on the perspective and background of the viewer.

The history of the latest half-century has increased awareness of the promises and difficulties of diversity. The ongoing European integration process has brought different cultures closer to one another. Exchange programs have increased awareness of national and cultural diversity. Migration makes major claims on communication skills and the ability to live as good neighbors with people who are perceived to be different while at the same time revealing xenophobia as a not-uncommon attitude in modern, rich societies.

In this situation two tendencies in the religious landscape appear as prominent: so-called secularization on the one hand and the so-called return of religion on the other. Many people have become used to secularization expressing itself primarily as indifference to religious issues and religious rites. People just do not care. However, since the early 2000s, we have seen a new tendency emerging, namely an atheism that is sometimes aggressively expressed. Significant inspiration has been found in authors such as Richard Dawkins (b. 1941), Christopher Hitchens (1949–2011), and Daniel Dennett (b. 1942).

With this new visibility of religion and the new atheism, we experience two seemingly contradictory tendencies that take place more or less simultaneously. I believe that they are parts of one and the same dynamic.

In September 2006, the German magazine *Der Spiegel* dedicated a special issue to the return of religion: "Weltmacht Religion. Wie der Glaube Politik und Gesellschaft beeinflusst" ("World Power Religion: How Faith Affects Politics and Society"). The issue was clearly a success, since it was translated into English in its entirety. This might have made Swedish journalists raise their eyebrows somewhat—many of them were trained in a spirit that expected the disappearance of religions or at least their complete marginalization. There are consequently very few journalists today who have good knowledge of theology, rites, and religious structures and denominations. As the writer Ylva Eggehorn has observed, during the last decades of the twentieth century, Swedish literature has been "saturated with theology in a very extraordinary way. ... But this is rarely reflected in reviews; a lack of knowledge of faith issues has long been a merit of 'modern' journalists." Sports and science journalism as well as financial coverage are doing far better in that sense. In those areas, the demand for expert knowledge is taken for granted in ways that theology and faith communities can only dream of.

Even so, the presence of religion in the media has increased considerably. The funeral of Pope John Paul II in 2005 was a media event of hitherto unknown extent. It seems that religious leaders and religious ideas have been accorded far more media attention recently. Within the framework of the international World Values Survey, sociologists speak of a growing interest in existential issues. Even newspapers have taken notice. In its presentation of a report that Danish futurologists had delivered, a Swedish daily shared:

> Between the years 1995 and 2004 the number of newspaper articles that included the word "God" increased by 234 percent, the Institute for Futurology in Copenhagen claims in its report "Religion-Future." Texts that included the term "faith in God" increased with as much as 3033 percent. As in Denmark, so also in Sweden. The periodical *00-tal* recently noted that God is very present in contemporary Swedish poetry. Modernization has not led to atheism, but to a lush private religiosity, in which everyone is his or her own bishop.

A Swedish Radio presenter noted, "During the ten years that I have worked with programs like People and Faith and the Philosophical Room, I have seen how interest in religion has increased all the time. There is a paradox in that people are not as interested in the churches as they are in the theological issues." And a press release from Swedish Radio said, "Theology engages people as never before." That seems to be confirmed by the fact that the theology festivals that have been held at Uppsala since 2008 have gathered some thousand participants each.

So far, one half of the dynamics. Now to the second half. In May 2007, *Der Spiegel* returned to the theme of religion, this time with the news bill "Gott ist an allem schuld! Der Kreuzzug der neuen Atheisten" ("It is all God's fault! The Crusades of the new Atheists"). In a series of articles, the Briton Richard Dawkins was presented as "the Pope of the New Atheists." The Frenchman Michel Onfray (b. 1959) and the already-mentioned British-American Christopher Hitchens together with the Italian Piergiorgio Odifreddi (b. 1950) were mentioned as the banner carriers of this crusade. The text gives the impression that (natural) science and religion are each other's opposites, not to say enemies. The pictures reinforce the message: advanced brain research in contrast to ecstatic believers, a biochemist in his laboratory in contrast to Hindu pilgrims. The summary claims that the high

GOD IS GREATER

priests of this crusade are natural scientists, authors, and philosophers.

The dynamic between the return of religion and the atheist crusade—to borrow the rhetoric of *Der Spiegel*—creates interesting challenges, not least for philosophers, theologians, sociologists, and anyone who is interested in interdisciplinary knowledge, especially in the relationship between the natural sciences and theology. We see, on the one hand, a growing interest in existential and religious issues, often in combination with a great lack of knowledge about religious traditions—in the Europe of today, both in the east and in the west, we have entire generations who have grown up in more or less religious alienation. On the other hand, we see new, furious attacks on religion. They are not always presented at the same intellectual level as the Uppsala philosopher Ingemar Hedenius (1908–1982) once did in his book *Tro och vetande* (*Faith and Knowledge*, 1949), but with much greater prophetic zeal. By and large, the message is that religion is irrational, rigid, and inclined to violence, and therefore it represents a danger to society and should be combated.

Richard Dawkins, the author of the book *The God Delusion,* was asked in an interview by an American daily paper, "If you could imagine a world without religion, what would it look like?" He replied it might look like modern Sweden. You can of course view it like that. However, the fact remains that a large majority of the population of Sweden are still in the 2010s members of a church.

Concurrently with the emphasis on the growing importance of religion expressed by various voices, the criticism of religion also increases in strength. Countless letters to the editor and publications of books testify to this. *God Is Not Great*, by Christopher Hitchens, is the title of one of these books that is critical of religion (2007). It is useful to be reminded that religion can have very negative and harmful effects. Religion has enormous power because it is concerned with what ultimately concerns us. If things go wrong, they often go terribly wrong. Not least we Christians are painfully aware of that.

Even so, it is misleading to judge religion only from the perspective of its adverse sides. To do so is like looking from a garbage-bin perspective. It is a bit like judging an entire family only on the basis of the content in their garbage bin. Even though, archeologically speaking, investigations of old garbage bins tend to be very rewarding, it is usually only as a jigsaw piece in the whole image that has been formed by other sources of knowledge as well. That is something quite different from judging an entire household as if its only function was to produce refuse. How fair could such a description of life be?

Criticism of religions should not be ignored. It contributes to keeping religious movements and institutions vigorous and self-critical. But it is also important to disclose it as a garbage-bin perspective whenever it is that. *God Is Not Great* is intended as a provocation, particularly against Muslims. A better book to write might have been *Religion Is Not Always Great, but God Is Greater*—a creed that both Christians and Muslims could agree on.

Fiction as the Seismograph of Secularization

In order to understand the dynamics between the new visibility of religion and the attacks of atheism, we could choose to take a closer look at polemical literature, but I would rather suggest a short, rhapsodic outing into the world of fiction, which I believe gives us a better picture of the interplay between faith, secularization, and atheism.

The German-Austrian author Daniel Kehlmann (b. 1975) has already as a young man put himself on the international literary map. His book *Die Vermessung der Welt* was published in 2005 (in English, *Measuring the World* in 2006). There he portrays two giants of science, each of whom has made major contributions to the Enlightenment: the scientist and explorer Alexander von Humboldt (1769–1859) and the mathematician Carl Friedrich Gauss (1777–1855). These giants of science devoted themselves literally to measure the size of planet earth—to establish its measurements—and they did so with extraordinary capacity and commitment.

I believe that the secret behind the success of this novel is that it is written in such an entertaining way with irony as a prominent feature. One reviewer noted that these "super humans," Gauss and Humboldt, gradually become similar to a couple of clowns. You can read the whole book as a radical but liberating criticism of Western worship of pure, incorporeal reason and the superstitious faith in the civilizing power of science. The screamingly funny corporeality constantly plays tricks with pure reason and turns it into a very human reason—into a part of what is human, or even all-too-human, and sometimes even into a game for those with worldly power, the far-too-powerful ones. This novel is hardly a contribution to a debate about religion and atheism, but through its ironic criticism of reason, it creates openings that are just as difficult for abstract theism as they are for abstract atheism. Far too many people believe that their own personal habits are basic rules for the world, as Gauss points out on one occasion. These habits also include prejudiced opinions about science and faith.

Swedish literature varies in its relationship to faith and spirituality: sometimes it is locked in conflict, sometimes a tension develops. Now and then there is a confusion of concepts. The foreword to the novel by Lina Sjöberg, *Resa till Port Said* (*A Trip to Port Said*, 2005) says, "Lina Sjöberg, born in 1973, is a postgraduate student at the Institute of Theology at Uppsala University, but her novel is no exercise in preaching Christian ideas. Rather, it is about ethics." Possible prejudice against the broadmindedness and skills of theologians is not up for comment here. But the fact that a novel that includes God, the Bible, a priest, and faith issues has to be provided with a content warning to say that it is not about anything Christian, but about ethics, suggests that things often become somewhat spasmodic when there is talk of religion. Phobia and blindness with regard to religion have a strong sounding board in Swedish cultural life. Ethics is passable; preaching is suspect.

In his novel *Norrlands Akvavit* (*The Aquavit of Northern Sweden*, 2007), Torgny Lindgren (1938–2017) drives the tension between secularization and faith further than many others. At a superficial level, the story is about a transition from revivalist faith to a modernity that needs neither God nor faith or religion. But *Norrlands Akvavit* goes much deeper. It also describes the transition from doubt to a faith that integrates the very opposite of faith itself: only as an apostate it is possible to find the way home. The fact that this novel makes that paradox visible is for me its most fascinating feature.

Norrlands Akvavit is the story of the revivalist preacher Olof Helmersson, who, after half a century, returns to the region where he once converted people to Jesus. But this time he comes to de-Christianize it, since he has come to realize that there is neither God, nor heaven or hell. Things do not work out the way he had imagined, though. In a way, this region has already de-Christianized itself. The shop assistant at the alcohol-monopoly shop at Skellefteå, says about her hairdo: "When I was very young, I belonged to a congregation where we all had this kind of hair bun.

GOD IS GREATER

All who had been saved. I soon got rid of salvation. But I kept the hairstyle." When Helmersson, on a bus journey, passed the place that used to offer a view of a prayer chapel, he says, "How strange! I could not see the chapel." "It burned down," the bus driver answered, "and nobody has bothered to build it up again."

The longer Helmersson stays, the more the paradox thickens: "What he thought or said in his own heart was, he explained, nobody else's business . . . that was a matter between himself and the God who does not exist." One of those whom Helmersson had converted half a century ago stated, "I myself do not believe, but I lack doubts. . . . Now we believe whatever we like. And on our own. That is part of our greatness." In the end, Helmersson summarizes his mission. "There is no eternity," he says. "That is why I have come back. I must put things right. And deny things. Everything. Before we all move on into eternity."

The thought is striking: it is only as apostates that we can find our way home. The newly gained experience of salvation does not last. It didn't for the psalmists of the Bible, and it didn't for Helmersson's new converts either. For most people, the way to maturity goes through the bitter moments of doubt. The paradoxes in *Norrlands Akvavit* remind us of a tension that is central to Lutheran theology. Its astounding formula, *simul iustus et peccator,* articulates the view of the human person as simultaneously righteous and a sinner, that he or she has simultaneously come home and become an apostate. It describes a dynamic that can lead to deep human maturity. It has to do with the authenticity of faith.

The books by the Brazilian author Paulo Coelho (b. 1947) often appear on international bestseller lists. His novels breathe an interest in spirituality and can also be seen as a plea for spirituality without formal religion. Coelho likes to choose Europe as the setting for his novels, and he seems to have a preference for travel, even for pilgrimages of an unconventional kind. Desert landscapes and dreams are important components of his stories. In deserts and dreams, his characters often have encounters with themselves or others that point them in new directions.

Those who admire Coelho praise his ability to make his readers open up to existential issues. Some think that he sets them free to encounter sublime aspects within themselves. Others are fascinated by the ambiguous ways in which Coelho depicts the interplay between facts and magic. However, what is brilliant,

GOD IS GREATER

wise, deep, and inspiring in the eyes of his admirers is (as is so often the case) only simplistic nonsense in the views of his critics.

Coelho's international breakthrough came with the novel *The Alchemist* (1988). What was then a fairly harmless potpourri of dreams, signs, and legends developed into a full-scale alternative spirituality in his later book, *The Witch of Portobello* (2006). The main character was born by a Romani mother at Sibiu in Transylvania. She was adopted by a well-to-do Lebanese couple, eventually ended up as a refugee in London, and worked as a real estate agent in the desert landscape of the Middle East. Athena, as she called herself, is a pilgrim, but of a special kind. As a believer, she is condemned by the established church: the Roman Catholic Church excommunicates her when she divorces her husband. Being an intelligent, gifted young woman, she slides away into what is called witchcraft: dance sessions that lead to a trance, initiation rites, clairvoyance, and a fusion of her own identity with "the great mother."

This novel engages in polemics against established religion, in this case against Christianity, which is experienced as rigid and dogmatic. The established religion presents itself more through what it does not want and what it is against than by affirming something or someone. Above all it appears as both anti-intellectual and anti-spiritual. It is anti-intellectual because it clings to reflections of worldviews that belong to the past. It is anti-spiritual because it suffocates authentic spiritual hunger by forcing it into predetermined templates. Witchcraft appears as a way out—as a way toward liberty beyond intellectual and spiritual straitjackets.

In this story Coelho gives a picture of Europe wrestling with its own intellectual and spiritual heritage. This wrestling appears as an individual process marked by interest in one's own spirituality and by criticism of established forms of religious community. You could also say that this is about the attempt to understand in depth the connection between spiritual and intellectual knowledge and wisdom, respectively.

The dialogue on these matters has made excellent progress over the last fifty years or so (more on that in the next chapter). However, Coelho's writings reveal something to which the theoretical dialogues between religion and science have not paid sufficient attention. Understandably, this work has been aimed at making things fit intellectually. That is an inescapable requirement. But Coelho's novels show that even more is required. There is a need and a longing to make life coherent, even in a spiritual perspective—and to make spiritual and intellectual aspects mutually interrelated, so that they complement rather than contradict one another. In other words, there is an irresistible craving for a view of life that is never less than rational but at the same time aware of the limitations of rationality—and which therefore includes something more than what is rational without thereby becoming irrational.

This is not an easy task. There are numerous examples of failed attempts, but only very few who have managed to mold a creative relationship between the intellect and spirituality. Many writers end up in either the one ditch or the other. Authors such as Danah Zohar (b. 1945) and Fritjof Capra (b. 1939) have wanted to turn quantum physics into mysticism, whereas authors such as Daniel Dennett and Richard Dawkins have sought to drown the spiritual child in the bathwaters of rationalism. Neither of these would attract Athena, the intelligent and well-educated person who seeks a wholeness in which both rationality and spirituality can find space and grow together.

This day and age needs a perspective on life that provides a positive challenge for individuals who are well educated, who want to live a life independent of authoritarian structures, who feel skeptical toward a cold and disembodied rationality, and whose primary criterion is something like "the truth is what feels right to me." With Søren Kierkegaard's (1813–1855) terminology, this would be people who are at the aesthetical stage—who have adopted a view of life that as such is respectable but who have not yet reached what Kierkegaard calls the ethical and religious stages. These people have developed an equally deep skepticism toward radical rationalism as they have toward radical secularism. They are often also very suspicious of what they perceive as traditional religion. And at this "aesthetical level" they keep their doors open, maybe for lack of better alternatives, to what in intellectual circles often—and quite rightly—appears as frighteningly irrational. In spite of the wonderful description of spiritual thirst, we see in Coelho a disconcerting tendency for alchemy to prove victorious over chemistry, magic over physics, astrology over astronomy, and phrenology over physiology.

Secularization, the New Atheism, and the Enlightenment

Secularization is no unambiguous phenomenon that can be grasped by simple explanations. It is no longer possible to say that religion will be almost automatically abolished in a modern society, nor that faith will be forced to take a step backward by every step forward made by science and technology. Today we can observe the emergence of new thinking about the relationship between secularization and modernization. We have also understood that secularization is not the primary enemy of Christianity but rather a consequence of Christianity itself, at least in parts. The empowerment of the world that follows from a Christian theology of creation makes space for secularization. Christianity has not only provoked the emergence of various views of life, it has also tolerated them and engaged in dialogue with them—and has thus contributed to the development of dialectic thinking.

Even the concepts of private and public are in the process of being redefined with regard to religion. *Private* refers to that which only very rarely concerns anyone else. There is a difference between private and personal. *Personal* refers to that which can be shared with others in a conversation in such a way that the sharing enriches everyone who participates and listens.

Faith is not private. Faith is personal. It is good to remember that *private* derives from the Latin *privare*, which means "to deprive." The community is deprived of what is private—most obvious when you hang out a sign that says "Private: Access Prohibited." Faith is personal, intended to enrich community and society.

Faith is a deeply personal matter and also deeply public because it forms our identity and our values. These are expressed in our private and personal lives, and in what each of us can contribute to the wellbeing of public life. The Old Testament prophet Jeremiah encouraged his compatriots who were refugees in Babylon to make every effort to help the city in which they were living to flourish: "Seek the welfare of the city where I [God] have sent you into exile, and pray to the Lord on its behalf, for in its welfare you will find your welfare" (Jer 29:7). Even so, people like to say that religion should be private, and only private. This is often claimed with a dogmatism that is puzzling, since it usually appears with those who are most critical toward religious dogmatism.

And how common such an attitude actually is, is questionable. Scholars of religion claim that today we can, quite to the contrary, observe a "deprivatization" of religion. This is partly a consequence of migration and globalization, which have made religion emerge more clearly as a mark of ethnic and cultural identity. To speak with the Spanish-American sociologist of religion José Casanova (b. 1951), we can see that religion is deterritorialized, and denominations are becoming internationalized: the religions are becoming more equally spread across the world, and denominations that once began in a limited area can now be found in many countries.

During the Reformation period, the religious peace treaty at Augsburg in 1555 formulated the rule *cuius regio, eius religio*: the ruling prince should determine which religion should apply in his country. That reality has now finally become undermined. In our day and age, religious denominations have really become global. National churches have developed more and more into anachronisms. The Church of Sweden is a name that stands for such a large capital of trust that there are good reasons to stick to it—a strong brand, as it would be called in commercial language—but theologically speaking, "Evangelical-Lutheran Church in

Sweden" would be a better expression of the identity of the Church of Sweden.

Our own time is also marked by the presence of large groups of people who, in the words of another sociologist of religion, Grace Davie (b. 1946) from Great Britain, could be described as "believing without belonging." They have a religious faith, but they do not feel any institutional belonging. This need not come to such dramatic expressions as it does in *The Witch of Portobello*, but it is a fact that we should take into account. At the same time, yet another sociologist of religion, Danièle Hervieu-Léger (b. 1947) from France, notes that there is also a great deal of "belonging without believing": it is possible to belong to a denomination without actively sharing its faith. These phenomena are far from unambiguous, but they do make it harder to arrange a tidy division between a public space that should be kept free of religion and a religious sphere that should be kept exclusively private.

Secularization led to criticism, and to the undermining and partial abolition of authoritarian religious institutions. With secularization, the era in which the church was part of the power apparatus has come to an end. At the same time, the insight is growing that the new visibility of religion might be of greater significance than the end of the church that represented the powers of authority.

This makes room for new public discussion on cultural, political, and philosophical ideas. In Sweden, the Humanist Society has made its voice heard in this debate. The word *humanism* has a broad meaning, of which the link to atheism is relatively new. Humanism in the traditional sense is primarily characterized by a strong interest in knowledge but also by its focus on humanity as the norm.

Humanism is more or less contemporary with the Reformation. In Europe, north of the Alps they both went hand in hand. The Reformation became an educational movement. Its great educationalist Philipp Melanchthon (1497–1560) was called "the Great Humanist." When the Humanists describe humanism as a "secular—non-religious—view of life which deems that there are no rational reasons to believe in any religious dogmas," the definition deviates on a number of significant points from previous, time-honored language. It also differs markedly from the self-understanding of the Swedish Humanist Association, founded in 1896, and from the Society for Christian Humanism, which came about in 1971 by an amalgamation between the Swedish Society for Christian Humanism and Social View (founded in 1918) and the Society for Christian Humanism (founded in 1937).

There are similarities between a humanist and a religious agenda. A Christian could sign up to much of the humanist action plan. It is of course very possible to be a nonreligious humanist, but it is just as possible to be a believing humanist (in the traditional sense of the word). You could even say that Christianity and humanism need one another in order to remain vigorous. Humanism reminds Christianity of its relationship to the universally human—it is philosophy's reminder that Christianity must never become a matter only for insiders, and the church must never become merely a club for mutual admiration. Christianity reminds humanism that concentration on humanity, even on universal humanity, gets it wrong when it degenerates into mere human navel gazing and forgets the rest of the world and creation.

When you read the program declaration of the Humanist Society, it is striking how strong a belief in reason it reveals. If people are only allowed to be reasonable and if they are liberated from "religion and all other forms of superstition"—as Christer Sturmark (b. 1964) calls these traditions of faith in his book *Tro och vetande 2.0* (*Faith and Knowledge 2.0*, 2006)—many problems will find their solutions.

A look at history shows that it is not as easy as that. It is of course right that the philosophy of rationalism has contributed a great deal to furthering science and to the emergence of human rights. But rationalism has no more than Christianity or any other religion been able to protect humanity from violence and atrocities, whether these have been executed in the name of revolution or colonialism. Atheist rationalism does not appear to be a very promising cure against war and injustice. Even a rational human being becomes guilty. And guilt and shame are experiences that include more than reason, and they require reconciliation and a healing that surpasses what reason can provide.

Both reason and faith are strong forces that can work miracles when they are at their best, but they can also lead to catastrophes when they go astray. Use and abuse are always very close to one another. Science and religion have achieved brilliant results while atrocious crimes have been committed in their names at the same time. Precisely for that reason, criticism and self-criticism are needed all along the line. And just because of that, it seems strange that humanists have been so skeptical toward the institutions in society where critical and self-critical reflection on the theory and practice of religion should take place, that is, the university departments of religious studies and theology.

Common terminology varies somewhat with regard to religion and theology. By *religion*, I mean the ways in which faith finds expression in matters such as Holy Scriptures, rites, institutions, and historical or individual experiences. By *theology* I mean a critical and self-critical reflection on the content and effects of a religious tradition. It would seem that not everyone who makes a statement about theology believes that theology is, or even can be, both critical and self-critical. It also seems that people do not think they necessarily need to have any particularly deep knowledge of theology in order to express quite a specific opinion of it.

The most serious aspect of the new atheists, however, is not that they are quite happy to construct a prejudiced caricature of religion as irrational, tending toward violence and conflicts, rigid and caught up in a prescientific worldview with a dualism between the natural and the supernatural as its primary feature. It is more serious that the alternative they are launching is a rehashed form of European Enlightenment philosophy. The program of the atheist humanists is quite simply not sufficiently radical to encounter the challenges that humanity is facing. Old-fashioned enlightenment thinking is not enough. Our globalized and technological era requires more than reheated Western leftovers.

The new era, which, following the eighteenth-century Enlightenment was to overcome faith by reason and in that way to replace prejudice by tolerance and create societies without discrimination, never arrived. Today it is a reasonable assessment that a mutually critical and self-critical relationship between faith and science is far more useful to humanity than confrontation.

I am not saying this in order to diminish the importance of the Enlightenment period. The basic ideas of the Enlightenment represent significant values. That people use their own reason independently is a presupposition for visions of freedom and a good society to become a reality. Progress is not possible without reason.

The Enlightenment philosophers thought that the light of reason would dispel all darkness. The aspect of freedom becomes obvious in Immanuel Kant's (1724–1804) definition of the Enlightenment as humanity's emergence from self-imposed immaturity. Kant powerfully launched the motto of the Enlightenment period, *Sapere aude*—have courage to use your own reason! Dare to know!

The philosophy of the Enlightenment put its trust in human autonomous reason as its firm anchor in life. Reason was thought to have the ability to analyze and criticize just about everything. There was stature and human dignity in that view, and the fruits of science that it has rendered cannot be overestimated. But there is a significant objection to that way of thinking, and that opens with the question: How autonomous is reason actually?

At one point Enlightenment thinking did not go far enough in its criticism. It did not want to, or was not able to, criticize reason itself, to which it referred with such emphasis. A corrupt and wavering reason has no place in the Enlightenment. But it is nevertheless a well-documented fact in real life.

The thought of autonomous reason and the human person as an autonomous subject has been criticized and undermined by both philosophers of science and social pragmatists. The pendulum has sometimes swung a bit too far to the other side: the personal and social identity of a human being has been reduced to a social construction. But the knowledge that actually arrived with the Enlightenment and stayed includes the insight of how important it is to analyze the way in which knowledge is connected to power, and how the supposedly private and inner life that we call religion is also always public and political.

These insights can help us come to terms with the Eurocentric patterns of interpretation inherent in the Enlightenment philosophy and can make the European traditions of ideas fruitful in a new way in the global arena. They will also contribute to overcoming the elements of the Enlightenment view of the human that appear to be obsolete in the light of modern research—including theological research. A criticism of religion that is based only on the concept of reason from the Enlightenment period is not sufficient. It is too black and white for today's multicolor palette of life.

How Postmodern Are We?

To a great extent we have let go of the thought that reality is basically static, and we have started to consider it as dynamic instead. Space, time, and language determine how we perceive reality. Reason is not unaffected by what it understands; it is also formed by its own context. It has become less autonomous and more contextual, you might say.

That does not mean that everything is relative. It is still fully possible to express oneself with exact precision. To use the contextualization of reason as a cover for all kinds of irrationality would be a serious mistake. The contextual concept of reason provides access to several perspectives but does not offer any excuses to cheat with regard to intellectual accuracy.

This is a lesson we have learned from twentieth-century physics in particular. Neither the theory of relativity nor the uncertainty principle of quantum physics can be taken as a pretext for lowering the requirements for rationality. Sharpness of thought is needed nowadays just as much as in the past. The requirements of rationality are indispensable. The *sapere aude* of the Enlightenment applies with undiminished strength, even at a time when we have realized that reason is always embedded in and related to a context. Maybe it applies to an even greater extent at the moment. *Sapere aude*—have the courage to think for yourself, and in more than one dimension!

Modernity has matured. Today we have by and large left simple, scientific-positivist ideas behind, and we have learned to understand that mixture, complexity, and hybridity are characteristics of the air that we breathe. We have become more interested in the composites and the particulars than in the monolithic and universal. You could say that today we expect more insight from investigating the seams that hold together the clothing of knowledge that dresses our civilization than just being blinded by this dress in all its glamour.

With regard to philosophy and theology, our growing familiarity with voices from contexts other than the West has opened our eyes to recognize just how complex our own tradition of ideas actually is. Asian, African, and Latin-American theologians have for example made us aware of the fact that there has never been any *theologia absoluta et pura*, any absolute and pure theology in which foreign elements have constituted heretical exceptions. The "normal" state would rather be that theology works with language that can motivate and nourish hope. And that does not take place through a theology that is *absolute* but through a theology that is *resolute* in its critical and self-critical reflection on the content and effect of the tradition of faith. Such a theology takes on elements from other contexts. It always has traits of syncretism—or in a less negatively loaded word, there is an inevitable hybridity in theology. It has been like that from the very beginning, when Christian theology emerged in conversation with Greek philosophy, even though there always are and always have been attempts to make this hybridity invisible.

It is often said that our own day and age is postmodern, that it no longer accepts either the view of knowledge of the premodern era (in which the power of the church over thought is usually routinely emphasized) or the scientific alternative (but just as absolute and equally routinely perceived) claim to be able to explain everything. Postmodernism, it is thought, criticizes all types of great, world-explanatory narratives—the so-called metanarratives. In a postmodern perspective, nothing is true in general—whenever anything has been considered as true, it has been done within the framework of a given historic context. In that sense, almost all truths are human constructions that build on the given presuppositions of a particular time.

Today there is a wide spectrum of interpretations of postmodernism. The views differ as to the extent that everything is a construction. Sometimes postmodernism is rejected as academic luxury talk, and sometimes it is combated as a social danger that, it is feared, might lead to the dissolution of all truth and morals. I myself would plead for a constructive interpretation that in summary says: not everything is a construction, but just about everything presents itself to us as embedded in constructions—and that also applies to postmodernism itself.

Postmodern criticism questions the old metanarratives and their claim to universal validity. But it can never govern the emergence of metanarratives, and ever since the Second World War we have seen the emergence of at least two new, extremely strong such narratives. One of them emerged through the atomic bomb and is about the ability of humanity to exterminate itself through the power of arms. The second narrative is about the climate of the earth. That too is truly global and concerns the survival of humanity and the planet. Supposedly, digitalization qualifies as a third one.

If these deliberations about secularization, the new atheism, the Enlightenment, and postmodernism are more or less correct, it is possible to conclude that what we need is a harder enlightenment and a softer view of truth. That means undiminished demands on intellectual honesty but greater humility. That implies an enlightenment that is enlightened about the danger of becoming rigid within one's own dogmas. It also implies a more open philosophy and theology that take seriously our vulnerability to the uncertainty that basically characterizes existence but also to the contextuality that makes it necessary for us always to translate between different texts and contexts.

This will have consequences for the way in which we talk and think about God. The Italian philosopher Gianni Vattimo (b. 1936) points out that in our time we have left behind the modern way of talking about God (theism). The question is no longer whether it is possible to argue in favor of God's existence but whether it is meaningful to talk about God. How can anyone ever believe in a God after Auschwitz?

In the wake of the 1960s God-is-dead theologies, new concepts have been born, such as "God is more than necessary," found in the works of the German theologian Eberhard Jüngel (b. 1934). The French theologian Jean-Luc Marion (b. 1946) speaks of a "God without being" and the American philosopher John Caputo (b. 1940) about "God as event." Thus theology has changed onto a different linguistic track. The arguments in favor of the reasonableness of God's existence (primarily based on Anglo-Saxon analytical philosophy) appear to be bloodless. It becomes all the more urgent to make links with a philosophy that is asking for a passionate God, a God in whom we might dare to hope.

Vattimo's point is that when postmodernism toppled theism, the foundation for the atheism that had presented itself as its opposite also fell away. The most important statement about God is no longer that God exists. Thus, the statement that God does not exist also loses its relevance.

There are, Vattimo stresses, three aspects of the atheist argument in particular that appear as hopelessly out of date: its epistemology, which is reminiscent of nineteenth-century unbridled optimism about science; its dualistic worldview, which was built on a contradiction between natural and supernatural; and its perception of God as a reflection of an earthly tyrant. At a time when so many opposites have ceased to appear as absolute, and interest is instead focused on the dynamic relation between them, it is atheism that has lost its theoretical foundation. That does of course not mean that we could say that God has been proved in any sense. But an atheism that is no more than reheated Enlightenment philosophy does not go very far. It does not bother to consider any new developments in the fields of philosophy and theology. It is not good enough in a globalized world, since it claims—fairly uncritically—that a European specialty possesses global validity. And it is not able to contribute to the spiritual readiness that we need to build up in view of the questions and challenges that humanity must begin to deal with for the sake of the entire planet.

The new atheism usually insists on considering faith as an inferior kind of knowledge. It is this view that governs and limits the arguments. It closes its eyes to the understanding of faith as a relationship of confidence and trust, and as a driving force for hope.

The German philosopher Jürgen Habermas (b. 1929) pointed to the fact that reason that takes self-criticism and its own limitations seriously cannot but go beyond itself toward an encounter with that which is something other than reason. Reason that is aware of its limitations will thus be inevitably interested in theology. It is in the interest of both philosophy and democracy to deal affectionately with the cultural and religious sources that nourish the awareness of norms in citizens and enable open and complementary learning processes, Habermas claims.

The Role of Theology in Our Day and Age

Theology both needs our contemporary public space and is needed within it. For its own sake, it needs to be exposed to transdisciplinary and public conversation. It is not possible to undertake any critical and self-critical work without relating beyond oneself. Major demands for quality and truth require constant reflection on the way in which conventional concepts and definitions interact with and within various public contexts.

That reflection also fulfills a necessary function of warning and protection with regard to possible abuses of religion. Just because religion can lead to catastrophic consequences when things go wrong, this public discussion is necessary. An open discussion provides better protection against degenerate variants of religion than a religiosity that is pushed aside into private rooms and isolated from public intellectual conversation.

Theology is also needed in society in many respects. Today we see new and often unexpected alliances being formed, such as between religious groups and environmentalists. The periodical *The Economist* reported already in 2007 how secular green and religious people often discover that they stand on the same side in public debate in many parts of the world. Sometimes they stand side by side hesitantly, and sometimes for tactical reasons, but it is often because they are driven by a sense of having something in common deep down.

The biologist E. O. Wilson (b. 1929), also a critic of religion, in the 1970s became known across the world through his book on sociobiology. He turned toward religion in one of his later books, *The Creation: An Appeal to Save Life on Earth* (2006), which is a letter addressed fictitiously to a Baptist pastor. The message is: "Pastor, we need your help. Creation is the glory of the earth. Let's see if we can't get together on saving it, because science and religion are the most powerful social forces on Earth. We could do it."

A similar argument has been put forward by the religious studies scholar Mary Evelyn Tucker at Yale University and one of the leaders of a project on world religions and ecology, which has resulted in a series of books published by the Harvard University Center for the Study of World Religions. Yale's School of Forestry has created a multidisciplinary research project on environmental changes that also looks at the role of religion and values in that context. In the article in *The*

Economist that I just mentioned, Tucker says, "Religions provide a cultural integrity, a spiritual depth, and a moral force which secular approaches lack." In order for collaboration to come about, it is not only committed faith but also qualified theological work that is needed. There is however a risk, at least in Sweden, that the fear of confessionalism might prevent the best theologians from being "socially useful" in this sense.

British scholars have investigated how so-called ordinary people discuss ethical issues. They concluded that the variety of religious themes that are included in this debate is underestimated and far too little explored. The questions that are asked very often have a religious dimension that is easily neglected by experts on science, politicians, and the media. Media often stamp deeply existential issues as subjective, emotional, or irrational chatting, while the experts usually stick to the technical aspects of one isolated issue at a time. Neither the one nor the other approach provides a satisfactory answer to the overall existential issues in which citizens are interested. In consequence, communication fails, and comprehensive public conversation does not happen—thus risking serious problems, since democratic society is dependent on functioning public communication. When the scholars investigated the communication on genetically modified food, they drew the following conclusion: "theological perspectives may now be indispensable in helping explain to largely secular institutions the sources and dynamics of conflicts now threatening to paralyze the development of what is being posited as a key technology for the twenty-first century."

If they are right, the public role of theology is not merely wishful thinking by a few of the faithful but actually a necessity for a well-functioning democratic society. While it is common in Sweden to claim that a democratic, multicultural society requires a neutral, religion-free public space, here is an argument for the opposite view: precisely because a democratic and multicultural society needs to function well, theological conversation is also needed in the public space.

With its doctrinal expressions and rites, religion is at the same time robust and changeable. In many areas, good proposals for solutions nowadays require collaborations between the best knowledge of the natural sciences, technology, the humanities, and theology. The new challenges create new alliances right across denominations and religions. They redraw the religious maps in a surprising, even bewildering way.

People of faith can recognize one another right across religious boundaries and can discover that they have far more in common with one another than with some parts of their own tradition.

After secularization, in between the new visibility of religions and the crusades of atheism, between the death of the old metanarratives and the birth of the new global narratives—how should we understand our own day and age? What we know for sure is that the picture is not unambiguous. And the clear-cut and unambiguous are not what we should strive for in our time. Simple explanations have played out their role. New conversations are possible. New patterns of action and new identities can emerge. Maps are being redrawn. There is always a risk in that, but also a well-founded hope.

3

Beyond the Caricatures: The Future Requires Well-Functioning Interplay between Faith and Science

The year is 2005. A hundred years have passed since Einstein formulated the special theory of relativity, and the centenary is celebrated by, amongst other things, a conference on Einstein, God, and Time at the Clarendon Laboratory at Oxford.

GOD IS GREATER

The distinction of the place inspires respect—I have spent my all and a little more on my lecture on "A Relativistic Eschatology" in order to do justice to both theology and physics.

In the evening of the same day, one of the most internationally well-known theologians of our time gives a popular science lecture on the same theme. After a short introduction on the jubilee itself, he moves on to painting one picture of the kingdom of heaven after the other, inspired by the book of Revelation. To my taste, it is too much piling words on top of one another and too little critical reflection in the light of modern physics and cosmology. I fear that his style of lecturing might diminish the respect of the scientists for theology and confirm the prejudice that "religion is only about a lot of old myths." You can guess at my surprise when, during the following mingling, I overheard some prominent physicists saying, "This was all so inspiring!" and "Thank goodness—at last a theologian who actually believes in God!"

Is it possible to unite faith and (natural) science? Or would it be best if they were kept apart? These questions are subject to much misunderstanding and wishful thinking. Some people take an interest in showing that faith and knowledge are each other's opposites. Some of them claim that faith ideas are lacking in rationality, that they contradict all logical analysis and therefore lack any value as truth. But as my conference experience at Oxford showed, there are those who find in that same contradiction a guarantee for the true value of faith. For them, faith becomes more authentic the more it militates against reason. As if it would be all the more noble to believe against reason than with reason!

Neither of these two positions is satisfactory. The consequences of the latter might even become bizarre. A Swedish physicist wrote to me: "I much prefer Åke Green, who does at least stand for something and pays the price. Much better than some leaders within the Church of Sweden!" *(Translator's note: Åke Green [b. 1941] is a Swedish Pentecostal pastor who was prosecuted but acquitted under Sweden's law against hate speech because of dehumanizing opinions on homosexuality in his sermons.)*

In a remarkable way, the longing to have irrational perceptions of faith forcefully presented unites some of the most committed defenders of the faith with some of its keenest slanderers. The physicist who was so assured of his faith would probably recognize himself in the atheist P. C. Jersild's (b. 1935) complaint in *Dagens Nyheter* *(Translator's note: a leading Swedish daily)*, "Unlike in 1949, when Hedenius had his battle with the bishops, there is nowadays very little to take hold of. The image of God can be so watered down that it reaches quite homeopathic dilution."

But can the motto "the less reason, the more spirituality" ever be viable? There are of course some religious groups that fit into this pattern. But many others shudder at that sort of attitude. The Lutheran tradition ought to be one of those that are least inclined to celebrate irrationality. The Reformation started on a university campus. The protection of intellectual honesty is a special responsibility for the Lutheran and Reformed traditions.

If it were the case that spiritual growth and maturity was primarily an irrational process, the gap between spirituality and a world that is to a great extent marked by the natural sciences and technology would be infinite. That would be disastrous. The problems that confront humanity today cannot be dealt with by dreamy subjectivity or superstition, but they can certainly be tackled by prayer united with rational action. Spirituality must never legitimize the choice of pseudoscience over science.

It is worrying that we currently observe a global increase of religious denominations that have a tendency to prefer the irrational. Many traditional churches have decreased in the number of their members. At the same time movements that favor authoritarian expressions of faith and that have only little interest in an equal dialogue between religion and science are growing stronger. Besides this, investigations made in the EU states also indicate that the more religious people profess to be, the less well informed they are about important social issues, such as biotechnology.

Why is it that people of faith hand over the most decisive discussions about the future of humanity and the earth to their agnostic or atheist fellows? That is a sin in the theological sense of the word. Something is wrong if the voices that associate spirituality and religion with irrationality and dogmatism are allowed to set the agenda. And it would of course be even more serious if it turns out that reality gives ample reason for such an interpretation. Faith and spirituality need rather to unite vision with rationality and social commitment. If there is a need for a new Enlightenment to safeguard science (not only the natural sciences), objectivity, and freedom, Christian people ought to take the lead. And it does seem as though such enlightenment is needed because it is a bad omen that, according to a report published in 2010, 21 percent of the population of Sweden believe that astrology is science.

There are misunderstandings and misconceptions, sometimes as a result of prejudice, that can trouble the relationship between faith and knowledge. Not least for that reason, this is an area in which it is fascinating, stimulating, and challenging to work—and above all urgent. To me, it looks like a triangular drama with science, faith, and the shared responsibility for the good of the world as the three parties.

Our *faith in knowledge* has again and again proved to be very effective. It is built on the conviction that the world can be described by the laws of science and that there is agreement between reality and our capacity to understand it. But there is also something that we could call *the knowledge of faith*—in which theological analysis and reflection are just as self-evident as spiritual experience and wisdom—that has had such a great influence on our view of the world and of life, our values and evaluations, and of their expressions in various cultural manifestations. How the triangular drama between the faith in knowledge, the knowledge of faith, and their shared responsibility for the world will develop is relevant to the most significant issues of humanity. Peace, a just sharing of food and water, the fight against epidemics, the increase of population, migration and climate—all these issues have aspects in which religious positions are significant. For the good of our society and of the world, a well-functioning dialogue and collaboration (*diapraxis*) between the faith in knowledge and the knowledge of faith is needed.

White Coats and Black Coats as Caricatures

The natural sciences and religion are two of the strongest forces that have shaped what we call our culture. For millennia, religion has not only attuned our mind to what is holy but has also formed our values and our social structures in such important areas as medicine and education. Art and music are also bearers of religious motifs to a great extent. And the natural sciences and technology have not only taken humanity to the moon—they are involved in virtually every dimension of life. That is why it is so urgent to look at how these two forces have stood and can continue to stand in a mutually critical relationship to one another.

Modern-day research into the history of the sciences has shown how theological and scientific thoughts have interplayed with one another in many different ways. The relationship between them is similar to the dynamics in a growing family. During the Middle Ages theology practically reigned supreme—as the queen of all the arts and sciences. The theologian Thomas Aquinas (ca. 1225–1274) created a powerful synthesis of the best of the available knowledge of theology, philosophy, and nature. His primary aid was the philosophy of Aristotle (384–322 BC), which had reached Christian Western Europe thanks to Muslim scholars.

The fact that the technique of measuring time received a good push forward through the monastic commitment to the Divine Office at regular times and that Protestants devoted themselves to clock- and watchmaking to a far greater extent than Roman Catholics are only two minor entertaining examples of the partnership between religious and scientific-technological know-how and culture. The latter fits well with Max Weber's (1864–1920) theory that Protestant ethics has been marked by a high degree of working morality and a well-considered use of time. In the seventeenth and eighteenth centuries, it was considered a good and urgent task to read and seek to understand both "the book of Scripture" and "the book of

Nature," and in many ways Christian theology created a propitious climate for the development of the natural sciences.

Sometimes people speak of "the ancient conflict" between science and religion. This ancient conflict is in fact a myth. A more truthful description is that science and religion have always done things for one another. To a major extent, they share each other's history, visions, discussions, and agonies. When the church father Tertullian complainingly asked in the third century, "What does Athens have to do with Jerusalem?" this question was precisely an expression of the fact that, already at that time, there was a lively exchange between the then-contemporary science (the natural philosophy symbolized by Athens) and Christian theology (symbolized by Jerusalem). And so it has continued. Many of the so-called modern natural sciences were pioneered by priests or persons who were close to the church in some other way. From the perspective of a Christian theology of creation, they saw reason as one of God's many good gifts and the scientific exploration of nature as a form of worship.

It is no coincidence that Galileo Galilei (1564–1642) thought it was like looking into the face of God when he directed his telescope toward the heavens, that Carl von Linné (1707–1778) thought he saw God on his backside in nature, and that the philosopher Immanuel Kant (1724–1804) considered that the starry sky above him and the moral law within him convinced him that there is a God. For Francis Bacon (1561–1626), who is often presented as a portal figure of scientific thinking, *scientia*, the realm of science, was synonymous with the realm of God.

The family relationships between theology and the natural sciences have of course not always been idyllic. Developments did not differ very much from what happens in ordinary families with teenagers. The dethroning of theology as the queen of the sciences and the emancipation of the natural sciences led to tensions. The conflicts around Galilei and Darwin are examples of this—even though it was in both cases about something else besides a conflict between religion and the natural sciences. But even though relationships might have been tense, it was never a case of a complete break.

During the twentieth century, the natural sciences and theology reached a more mature relationship. Some hurdles have been overcome. Logical positivism and scientism, which seek to reduce all knowledge to scientific explanations, have been successfully questioned. Theological indifference or arrogance in the face of the natural sciences has by and large been punctured.

A large number of books on the dialogue between natural science and religion in general have been published, as well as on the relationship between religion(s) and specific scientific disciplines and on various special issues. This dialogue has gained speed through a number of periodicals and through the work of various centers of dialogue and academic societies.

The physicist and religious studies scholar Ian Barbour (1923–2013) has described the relationship between religion and the natural sciences on the basis of four different models: *conflict*, *independence, dialogue,* and *integration.* The model of conflict is mostly built on misunderstandings and caricatures of what science and religion are and of how they work. It is therefore not fruitful.

Independence is a model that occurs quite frequently. Nevertheless, it is unsatisfactory in the long run. Simple distinctions, such as the natural sciences ask "how" but religion asks "why," do not stand up to closer scrutiny. How and why are asked in all quarters. Besides this, the independence model makes it impossible to reach any collaboration between the best knowledge in all available areas. I do not consider the integration model viable either; it is both unrealistic and undesirable. Unified totalitarian systems have turned out to be rather less than successful in the history of humanity.

Dialogue remains as the best alternative. That model is built on respect, both for the natural sciences and for theology as sophisticated areas of knowledge, on a fruitful tension that arises through differences in methods and areas of research, and on the experience of major overlap with regard to ideals of knowledge and intellectual honesty.

Resistance to dialogue often rests on prejudiced misconceptions on both sides. One such misconception is that the natural sciences function as a self-supporting household: it has all it needs within itself and provides a value-free home to pure knowledge that rests secure on the foundation of measurable observations. This perception is illustrated by the idea of the scientist in his white coat, who systematically reveals the secrets of nature below the world's strongest microscope. A similar misconception is that theology is by definition the same as dogmatism and indoctrination—a way of forcing on people something that claims to be the only truth, but that is in fact speculation based on revelations that lack any truth that can stand up to proof. You can imagine a person in a black coat who, with a sinister face, supervises that orthodox teaching is followed.

Both the white coat and the black coat are bad caricatures. It is not always very easy to get rid of the stereotypes that have shaped them, since they have a tendency to survive in more sophisticated forms—maybe even in the oversight of universities and high schools. When universities and the corporate sector collaborate in scientific research and education, it is often considered to raise the quality of education, from which both parties benefit. When universities and religious denominations collaborate in religious studies and theological research and education, the conclusion is however often drawn that the objectivity of the studies is under threat. Here the collaboration with the "consumers" quickly becomes a problem in principle.

Where is the difference? The corporate sector is by no means a space free of ideology, even though the awareness of this fact might vary considerably. In the area of religious studies and theology, great awareness of the influence of ideas and ideologies (for good or bad) is however inherent. Consequently, there is therefore a stable tradition of training in critical hermeneutics. Thus, the preconditions for critical and constructive collaborations with the agents in the future labor market of the students are therefore much better in religious studies and theology than in many other fields. The question merits asking: What is in fact behind the use of such different standards for the natural sciences and religious studies?

When the dialogue between science and theology does gather speed, it often turns out that it is not altogether easy to leave the simplifications and the prejudices behind—at least when it comes to prejudice about theology! Most people realize that expert knowledge is required in order to make statements about quantum theory or about the interpretation of the fantastic images that have been collected by the Hubble telescope. Far fewer people realize that expert knowledge is also required in order to discuss theology. Sometimes the prejudice becomes overly explicit: deeper knowledge of scientific models appears as a virtue, whereas deeper knowledge of theological models appears as an unnecessary detour. Mutual respect for one another's fields of knowledge is however a prerequisite for a well-functioning interplay.

The Story about the Balloon

I can remember quite a hot debate at the end of the 1980s between two prominent professors, the theologian Wolfhart Pannenberg (1928–2014) and the primatologist Christian Vogel (1933–1994). It focused on the relevance of theology for evolutionary biology. Pannenberg argued that God is a necessity for an adequate understanding of nature. Vogel claimed the contrary. His argument was in short that we can see that things work without God! At the height of the debate he exclaimed, "You say that there is a minute balloon somewhere out there, floating in a corner, that I must take into account in my work as a scientist here and now. I look and look, and I cannot even see that balloon. Why would I care in my scientific work about a balloon which in my view does not even exist?"

Pannenberg countered that if the God of the Bible is the creator of the universe, it is not possible to reach a full or even any approximate understanding of the processes of nature without reference to this God. But, on the contrary, if a complete or almost complete understanding of nature is possible without any reference to the God of the Bible, then God cannot be the creator of the universe and consequently God cannot really be God. And if so, we cannot trust God as a source of any moral knowledge either.

These were serious allegations on both sides. I felt great hesitation. Neither the self-righteousness of the scientist, who reduced theological issues to some insignificant little balloon somewhere out there, nor the foolhardiness of the theologian, who staked everything on just one card of the theory of knowledge, seemed a possible way ahead. I left the room with a strong conviction that neither of these starting points would hold water. The relationship between the natural sciences and theology must surely be richer and more complex.

What is wrong with Pannenberg's and Vogel's ways of thinking? To begin with, I think they both suffer from a deficient insight about dialogue and learning. In that debate, they both gave evidence of a perception that assumes that there is only one correct answer to be reached. This has a negative effect on the culture of questioning. From an epistemological point of view, there is much to be said for seeking to keep a culture of Socratic dialogue alive, such as it has been modeled for us in Plato's *Symposium*, for example. There the answer always keeps the door open for the next question. All who are interested in seeking truth must help to bring new knowledge to birth. With a phrase from Socrates (469–399 BC), whose mother is supposed to have been a midwife, we speak of the maieutic project of knowledge (from the Greek *maieuein*, "to deliver"): the teacher and scholar is seen in the role of a midwife who helps the process of giving birth. All our knowledge is preliminary to a greater or lesser extent. Even though we sometimes use the adjective *ultimate*, our collective knowledge of the world is only ultimate in a very small sense, and all the more preliminary.

In these circumstances, it is not very becoming for anyone to proclaim themselves as the only one in possession of the truth. And it is not only more becoming but also more realistic to take an interest in collaboration and interplay between different types and fields of knowledge. If I am right that science and religion are the forces that have influenced our culture the most, and that they are drawn into a triangular drama in which our faith in knowledge, the knowledge of faith, and the common responsibility for the world play the main parts, then theology can definitely not be described as an insignificant little balloon. And the other way around also applies, for the theologian can never consider the natural sciences as some little balloon far away out there that can be ignored without penalties.

Secondly, I believe that the story of the balloon testifies to a lack of historical insight. The relationship between science and theology has always been mutual and complex. It has quite often been possible to observe expressions of harmony and conflict at the same time. The lightning conductor is a good example. When it came into use, a tug-of-war emerged between various theological and moral positions. For some, the lightning conductor became proof that the use of the skills of reason that is pleasing to God leads to technological innovations that can save lives. For others, it was an example of human inability to leave things alone and a reprehensible attempt to improve on God's good creation. At a safe historical distance, we might smile at that discussion. On closer reflections, the arguments are not so very different these days. Is stem cell research a good use of humanity's gifts or an expression of human hubris that interferes with the basic code of human life without being able to consider the consequences realistically?

A long history of shared visions, agonies, and values suggests that the theological balloon is not stuck to any distant border of the cosmos of knowledge. It has in fact always floated across the waters of the creation of knowledge and has left considerable traces in the history of humanity.

Third, the story of the balloon reveals a naive view of knowledge. The natural sciences always act on the basis of certain assumptions about nature, which lie before all scientific research and do not permit themselves to be proved scientifically. To these belongs what Albert Einstein (1879–1955) called the great mystery that the universe permits itself to be explored. In that sense Einstein saw himself as an inevitably religious person, although he was not a believer in any distinct confessional sense—and he drew the conclusion that every serious human being ought to be religious, at least in that sense. In the entertaining book *Pythagoras' Trousers* (1995), the science journalist Margaret Wertheim (b. 1958) argued that research into the natural sciences from Pythagoras to Kepler, Newton, Boscovich, Faraday, Einstein, and onward has been nurtured by a religious faith in the unity of nature and a basic harmony—with "mathematical man" as the high priest of science.

Religious (and sexist) undertones surface also in Francis Bacon's view of nature as a wild woman, who had to be tamed and forced into submission. "I am come in very truth leading to you Nature with all her children to bind her to your service and make her your slave," Bacon proclaimed. For him, science appeared as a saint who gathers her faithful—the scholars—into monastic-like communities. A quick look at how the acquisition of knowledge works shows that multidisciplinary issues, including theological, do not permit themselves to be limited to some insignificant distant balloon, however large or little it might be. These issues exist in fact in the very air that both scientists and theologians breathe. Both these fields of knowledge have their own integrity, but they live in an atmosphere in which social and existential questions move freely across the subject boundaries. The balloon has been punctured, and the particles that filled it are scattered everywhere.

Fourth, the story of the balloon assumes quite a naive view of human beings. Neither the natural sciences nor theology can produce themselves. Both of them are pursued by people who are simultaneously very capable and very fallible. At the same time they both unite in the highest claims to deal with the questions of truth with the greatest integrity. Even though we might put aside spectacular scandals, such as the stem cell deception in Korea or sexual abuse in the church, we know that the ideals and the reality might be very far apart from one another. Scientists and theologians can hold one another accountable for living up to their own high standards. Both of them have ethical frames of reference that could strengthen one another. In that perspective, the little balloon is transformed into a tiny insect—into an irritating mosquito somewhere in the room that effectively prevents theologians and scientists from falling into the slumber of self-sufficiency.

At the end of the day, it is quite fascinating to see how many different lines of argument can be conducted about a balloon, which according to some people does not even exist. So the victory of reason over the stories of faith was not quite that simple after all! And it was not quite that simple to claim the necessity of God in the theory of knowledge. The necessity of God for knowledge and morals does not permit itself to be proved. God is something more and at the same time something less than necessary; God passes above the very category of necessity.

What Theology and the Natural Sciences Can Do for One Another

Pope John Paul II (1920–2005) was once asked what the natural sciences and religion and theology respectively can do for one another. His optimistic answer was that science can purify religion from error and superstition, and religion can purify science from idolatry and false absolutes. Each can draw the other into a wider world, a world in which both can flourish.

Today few theologians would seriously question that theology has much to gain from keeping up to date with scientific research and with the philosophy of science, even though action does not always follow the words. But is the opposite also the case? Does theology have anything to contribute to the field of science?

I think the knowledge of theology about the conditions, risks, and possibilities of interpretation is a rich source to draw upon. Theologians have great experience in hermeneutics—the theory and practice of interpretation. Hermeneutics takes seriously the fact that naked facts are far rarer than we are inclined to think. And even though it does happen that we encounter some naked facts, we immediately dress them up in our own language, our imaginations, our cultures, and the like. This process is entirely unavoidable given the brain structure that we live with. Hermeneutics contributes to bringing order in this often complicated process, which, when it goes wrong, can lead to misunderstandings and serious mistakes. It is quite a humble science that takes into account the possibility that we might never succeed in sorting out the ultimate truth.

These insights are highly relevant even in the fields of science, since theories and scientific terminology have ideological potential. Einstein complained about the ideological exploiting of the theory of relativity. The fact that time is relative in the physical sense cannot be taken as a pretext for general relativism. Quantum physicists have not only had to struggle with at least nine different interpretations of quantum theory; they have also experienced, time and time again, how people have sought to explain all sorts of implausibility with quantum theory. At an earlier stage of the history of science, the comprehensive explanation of the mechanics of the heavens in terms of gravity—that is, Newton's physics—led to an intensive search for unifying principles and structures in many other areas. In a similar way, the theory of evolution has stimulated the application of a general evolutionary perspective in widely different areas, often far removed from what can be said to be Darwin's understanding of evolution. Chaos theory and complexity research have also inspired popular fantasy to develop ideas that go far beyond the facts of scientific scholarship.

Words and concepts are not static; they move around in linguistic geography. Even scientific concepts sometimes become nomadic and take on new meanings in contexts that might be far removed from their original ones. Sometimes they return to their origin saturated with completely or partly different content. Such a process may lead to surprising consequences. It might seduce us into conclusions that have all but scientific foundations, but which nevertheless are dressed up in supposedly scientific apparel. Then the ideologization is a fact.

The philosopher of science Klaus Mainzer (b. 1947) carries out such a maneuver in his book *Symmetry and Complexity: The Spirit and Beauty of Nonlinear Science* (2005). He believes that symmetry and complexity are not only useful models for the natural sciences but that they are universal qualities of reality: "Since the earliest times nature itself has manifestly been a model, evincing regularity in sundry forms and occurrences—from the minerals and plants, to the anatomy of living beings, to the regularly recurring stellar constellations." From this, Mainzer draws conclusions about how we should relate to globalization: "Therefore, we should deregulate and support self-regulating autonomy," since "the sociodiversity of people is the human capital for a sustainable progress . . . in the evolutionary process of globalization." Regardless of one's own social-political view, the insight dawns that Mainzer moves ahead a little too rapidly when he deduces social and political norms straight from research in the natural sciences.

History shows that the potential for scientific concepts to create ideology is much more than merely a theoretical problem. Darwin's theories were further developed by his cousin Francis Galton (1822–1911) into the thought of improving the genetic quality of humans (eugenics), a step that led to tragic consequences in connection with the ravages of race biology in Europe and America during the last century. It can be hard to disclose the ideology when it is surrounded by an aura of scientific legitimacy. How easy it was for the church in Sweden to join race-biological research and in that way to legitimize abuse of the Sami people.

It is, in spite of all the difficulties that it implies, one of the tasks of Christian theology to keep alive a critical memory. In fact, such memory exists and is celebrated at the very heart of theology. At the center of the eucharistic liturgy we find the words of Jesus: "Do this in remembrance of me." That means, among other things, remember the crucifixion, and remember all incidents of injustice, in whatever name they are committed—but do also remember the resurrection, and proclaim in words and deeds a new justice and a new righteousness. I believe that theologians can contribute, without becoming self-righteous, to a sharper awareness of the everywhere-present risk of creating damaging ideology.

The Power of Metaphors

Metaphors are a fantastic invention. A metaphor is a linguistic image that "carries over" meaning. This is the verbatim meaning of the Greek verb *metapherein,* which in turn is the root of the word *metaphor.* Metaphors have a role to play in theology as well as in science.

A few years back I was planning a series of seminars on the theme "Ideas of Nature"—on different ways of looking at nature. My hypothesis was that views of nature have always been expressed by powerful metaphors—such as nature as an organism, as a body, as clockwork, or as a woman whose womb should be penetrated in order to achieve satisfaction—and that these metaphors have influenced the way in which different disciplines have related to nature. I therefore asked a cosmologist, a physicist, a biologist, a brain researcher, an anthropologist, and a psychologist to consider the following questions: What are the most common models and metaphors for nature that you use? How do they work? Have they been developed or criticized over time? Can you see any influence from religiously loaded thoughts on nature, for example that something is or ought to be holy? There were a lot of interesting contributions. In only one case did I receive the answer: You know, I don't really work with metaphors or ideas about nature, I only work with "the real stuff"—with nature itself.

Metaphors have always played a significant role in the natural sciences, both for the educational transmission of scientific knowledge to non-scientists and for the scientists' own understanding. In the words of the astrophysicist Alan Lightman (b. 1948), "Metaphor is critical to science. Metaphor in science serves not just as a pedagogical device ... but also as an aid to scientific discovery. In doing science, even though words and equations are used with the intention of having precise meanings ... it is almost impossible not to reason by physical analogy, not to form mental pictures, not to imagine balls bouncing and pendulums swinging. Metaphor is part of the process of science."

Metaphors transmit meaning and affect research and processes of understanding. The anthropologist Emily Martin (b. 1944) has shown that textbooks on immunology mainly use metaphors from the world of war. There is talk of battlefields, Blitzkrieg, mines, bombs that explode through cell membranes, executions, and so on. The body is seen through the metaphor of the national state that must defend itself against invasion. It is important to recognize the enemies and to eliminate them. Martin asks herself whether perhaps these war metaphors have had a hampering effect on the study of synergy effects in immunology. There is quite a difference if the framework of interpretation is borrowed from the war against terrorism à la George W. Bush or from the study of the mutual dependence of ecological systems. The framework of interpretation affects not only the understanding of existing data but also the formulation of the next research project.

Metaphors have always been part of the natural sciences. You might want to believe that they were more important in the past, when science was not as exact as it is today. Do an increasing specialization and more exact definitions not lead to the suspension of something as inexact as metaphors, which can then be dispatched to the curiosity cabinet of history? This has certainly happened to metaphors that have turned out to be badly chosen and misleading. However, the power of metaphors has hardly decreased for that reason. Maybe it has even increased. The more abstract the objects of science appear, the greater is the role that metaphors play. The more science seems to contradict our intuition, or the more distant its objects are from ordinary perception, the greater role do the metaphors play. Greater also is the risk that a badly chosen metaphor might cause some damage. This applies particularly to the physics, chemistry, and biology that work with the very large, the very small, and the very rapid—with cosmology, nanotechnology, and elementary particles. Alan Lightman has concluded: "It seems to me that metaphors in modern science carry a greater burden than metaphors in literature or history or art. Metaphors in modern science must do more than color their principal objects; they must build their reality from scratch. . . . We ought not to forget that when physicists say a photon scattered from an electron, they are discussing that which cannot be discussed."

Theologians recognize and are used to this kind of problem. A pregnant phrase for the experience that it creates can be found in the works of the famous theologian Karl Barth (1886–1968), who wrote: "As ministers we ought to speak of God. We are human, however, and so cannot speak of God. We ought therefore to recognize both our obligation and our inability and by that very recognition give glory to God." Theologians have gathered rather a lot of expertise in the field of metaphors. Many have developed a special sensibility here. Maybe it is even stronger than that of the philosophers, since theologians know that religious metaphors in particular have often achieved more good and more evil than many others.

Metaphors are thus no superfluous decoration. Nor are they an inferior form of knowledge that is waiting to be replaced by unambiguous, nonmetaphorical expressions. Rather, they have a positive value of their own. In their book *Metaphoric Process: The Creation of Sci-*

entific and Religious Understanding (1984), religious studies scholar Mary Gerhart and physicist Allan Russell definitely affirm that metaphors are creative and constructive rather than descriptive. They generate new worlds and new ways of orientating oneself within them. There hermeneutics provides invaluable help to orientate.

Philosophy Rather Than Theology?

The obvious objection at this point is: but why theology? Is philosophy not enough? Is that not even better? Because it seems more neutral, and, at least in Sweden, we have a preference for neutrality, or for what looks like neutrality.

Philosophy has undeniable merits with regard to the relationship between science and theology: it enables a metalevel, it offers a fairly neutral meeting place, and it is a decent judge when it comes to following the rules of good argumentation and fair dialogue. That is quite a lot, but it is not enough. There are at least three reasons to suggest that theology has something that philosophy does not have.

First, the type of critical reflection on which theology is an expert is needed whenever religious ideas and notions are involved. That applies to articulated as well as to implicit religious notions, but also to antireligious ideas and notions. The assertion that science has nothing to do with faith is therefore a statement that can and should be made the object of theological debate. Ethical and existential issues that arise in connection with science also have a theological dimension that should not be neglected. To these belong the so-called borderline issues and the eternal questions: What is the role of humanity? What can we know? What are we permitted to do, or what must we do? What may we hope?

Second, the perception that philosophy is completely objective rests on a number of problematic assumptions. It assumes that it is possible to distinguish between secular and religious reality in a way that also permits the declaration of a neutral sphere, and that what is neutral always applies universally and thus is more valuable than that which applies in a particular context. Finally it assumes that there actually is only one universal philosophy. All these assumptions have been called into question.

Third, questions about trust and trustworthiness affect theology and science in more or less the same way. People ask, Can you trust theology when it keeps changing (for example, to accept same-sex relationships)? Can you trust it when it does not change (but defends the *status quo* with reference to more-or-less isolated biblical quotations)? When it walks hand in hand with abuse of power, intrigues, and crises of trust? In a similar way, people ask, Can you really trust the sciences that always come up with new findings that seem to contradict one another? When limit values that have to do with our health seem to be changed for political of financial reasons?

My generation asked, Can you trust the natural sciences after the nuclear bomb? Can you trust the sciences after the research that was undertaken on prisoners in German concentration camps? What kind of science was it that could sanction that Jews, Romani people, black people, and people with disabilities were treated like beings that had not been created in the image of God? Today we wonder if we can trust the scientists with regard to genetically modified food, because where does the money for this research come from?

Questions about confidence and trust are often difficult and almost always complex. They include dimensions of faith, and thus they can be helped by theological analysis and reflection. Two more specific issues—one with a historical and one with a future perspective—will now illustrate these thoughts on the interplay between faith and science.

God and Darwin

Wherever there is some interest in describing the modern history of ideas as the victory of science over theology, reference is made to the controversies linked to the theory of evolution. These attempts are revealing in many ways, but they do not give any reason to picture Charles Darwin (1809–1882) as a crusader knight of scientism, or the representatives of theology as narrowminded inquisitors. The picture is far more exciting.

Darwin's book *On the Origin of Species by Means of Natural Selection* was published in 1859. That book revolutionized biology and turned human self-understanding upside down. The content was built on observations that Darwin had made almost three decades earlier, during his worldwide travels on the ship *Beagle*.

Darwin had hesitated to publish what is called the theory of evolution. He worked through all possible objections against it very carefully. And if his colleague and competitor Alfred Russel Wallace (1823–1913) had not been about to publish similar thoughts quite soon, the publication might have been delayed even longer. Darwin was aware that the theory of evolution would be controversial, both from the perspective of science and from the point of view of theology.

Some of the most challenging aspects were that geological research together with the theory of evolution would move the horizon of time away toward the incomprehensible. Up until then, the Christian world had read the history of humanity as a comprehensible chronicle of a family that could be contained within a few millennia, from the beginning with Adam and Eve, through all sorts of intrigues and a long chain of generations up until the present time. That story went bust!

Suddenly a few millennia became incomprehensibly many millennia, even millions and billions of years. The evolution of life appeared as a long process characterized by chance, adaptation, and natural selection. The forms of life had not been created as fixed and complete but had evolved over time and space. And humanity was no exception. Such upheaval would of course risk the self-confidence of human beings. A master that walks around in a top hat and feels that he is the crown of creation won't be very amused to learn that he shares his ancestry with the apes!

Various strategies were tested in order to come to terms with the enormous challenge of the theory of evolution for the intellect and the emotions. Some people condemned the new theory outright, and others sought to put together old and new ideas. Some even pleaded for an altogether new way of thinking and praised the grandness of the new evolutionary narrative. Spiteful attacks and cheeky caricatures were part of the picture. Darwin himself showed tolerance, humility, and self-criticism, both with regard to religious faith and the limits of science. He stressed that he had never been an atheist in the sense that he had denied God. However, the recognizably hard question of suffering and the love and almighty power of God made him an agnostic. It hit him with full force when his and his wife, Emma's, beloved ten-year-old daughter, Annie, died.

Later research has shown that there were remarkable differences between the ways in which the theory of evolution was received in various places in the world. The reception depended to a major extent on local, social, and political circumstances—it was rarely purely scientific reasons that determined how things went. At St. Petersburg, for example, where people were familiar with the study of the flora and fauna of

Siberia, there was from the beginning greater propensity to see collaboration rather than the fight for survival as the prime motor of evolution. In the southern states of North America, there were major difficulties concerning the common origin of all human beings. That the entire human race should have the same origin just could not be true, since that would question the ranking of the black and white races that was the basis of society there and then.

There were (and are!) those who believe that the theory of evolution is irreconcilable with faith in a creator God. The famous debate between the biologist Thomas Henry Huxley (1825–1895) and Bishop Samuel Wilberforce (1805–1873) at Oxford in 1860, and the formation of legends about the irreconcilable conflict between science and faith that have flourished in its wake, is an example of the way in which scurrilous portraits and wrongful popularizations can cause havoc for a serious dialogue between science, philosophy, and theology.

However, the conflicts are only part of the picture. Already in the year following the publication of *On the Origin of Species*, Frederick Temple (1821–1902) gave a sermon at Oxford in which he praised the progress of the sciences. This same Temple was later made the

Archbishop of Canterbury. There was no ecclesiastical opposition to the burial of Darwin in 1882 in Westminster Abbey. The nineteenth-century theologian Aubrey Moore (1848–1890) can stand as an example of a constructive reception of the theory of evolution. He considered that Darwin, under the guise of a foe, had done the work of a friend. According to Moore, Darwin was a friend because he made us expand the limits of an idea of God that was too small. He liberated theology from the image of God as a magician and helped to present the image of God who creates in, with, and under the natural processes that continue to progress. The "small" image of God turned out to be a faulty idea, even though it was common. Already the great Isaac Newton (1642–1727) had agreed with it: a God who created the world as a mechanical clockwork that rolls on by itself, by and large. Only occasionally, when it jams, does such a God put on his I-will-fix-it hat and adjust the mechanics. That is how we get the image of a God who only plays a role where human knowledge has gaps—a God of the gaps.

As the gaps of knowledge are filled in, one by one, such a God becomes both homeless and redundant. If God is only a supernatural being that pressed the button of creation once upon a time and then sits back to see how things go—and if God can only create by breaking the laws of nature—well, then we might as well agree with the new atheists: it is very unlikely that such a God exists. Such a God looks far too much like an enlarged image of a human engineer.

The theory of evolution, however, fits much better with an image of God in which God is greater than creation and at the same time involved in creation. A God who exercises creative powers through natural processes. A God who has allowed creation to bring forth human beings, who have become aware of the course of evolution and of their own history of development—people who can understand and experience themselves as God's created cocreators, who experience what is holy and who are aware of their own physical, mental, and spiritual skills and needs.

This perspective is breathtaking: on the one hand the insight that each one of us is almost nothing in relation to the vastness of the universe in time and space, and on the other hand the knowledge that we have so much power and responsibility for the life on this planet. On the one hand, often-brutal processes of development in accordance with the laws of evolution, and on the other the birth of individuals who experience freedom of thought and action, who constantly test the limits, and who express themselves in philosophy and frescoes, in music and poetry. Many centuries before Darwin opened his grandiose vision to us, a Jewish poet formulated this twofold experience: "When I look at your heavens . . . what are human beings that you are mindful of them, mortals that you care for them? Yet you have made them a little lower than God, and crowned them with glory and honor. You have given them dominion over the works of your hands" (Ps 8:3–6a).

Since the days of Darwin, the theory of evolution has influenced many other fields of knowledge while it has also continually developed further. This development has not been any straightforward story of success. The picture includes some sidetracks, such as the radical affirmation by social Darwinism for the rights and survival of the fittest and the devastating consequences of racial biology during the last century. In our own time the theory of evolution continues to develop through increased interest in research in the interplay between the conformity of nature to specific laws and freedom in the processes of development, and how collaboration at and between various levels constitutes a complement to the competitive struggle inherent in evolution.

The theory of evolution and its interpretations have given important contributions to the shaping of a modern view of the world, including the Christian view of the world. Our eyes have been opened to the rich variety of forms of life, to the flexibility in adaptation, and even to the hope for the future inherent in evolutionary thought. But we also see, attend to, and counteract the threats to life that emerge from the forces that drive evolution ahead. The path of evolution is lined with suffering, death, and the elimination of the weak. In our time we have more reason than ever to ponder humanity's own power to influence the possibilities and paradoxes of evolution. The latter are not altogether easy to solve, whether or not you have faith.

More than one theologian has shown that in many ways, Jesus had an anti-evolutionary message. Caring for the weak and love for the enemy challenges the principle of the maximized advantages of the best adapted. Here we still have much to talk about. A good starting point for such conversations could be the final words in *On the Origin of Species*. They have an irresistible brilliance: "There is a grandeur in this view of how life, with its several powers, having been originally breathed by the Creator into a few forms, or into one; and that, while this our planet has gone circling on according to the fixed law of gravity, from so simple a beginning endless forms most beautiful and most wonderful have been, and are being evolved."

It always takes time for us humans to digest new and overwhelming knowledge. That also applies to the sciences. It is well known that even a genius such as Einstein had major problems about accepting quantum theory, and in fact he never managed to do that. It also took time to incorporate Darwin's theory of evolution into general knowledge. It is still hard for us to understand the enormous periods of time we are talking about with regard to the world and the universe. The gap between our own lifespan on the one hand and millions and billions of years on the other hand is simply too great for our imagination to easily produce a coherent overall picture. This gap is a source of our intuitive skepticism against that which bursts our accepted frames of reference.

Intuitive difficulties of this kind, however, do not justify the myth about an eternal conflict between faith and knowledge. It is dangerous to cultivate this myth because it plays into the hands of extremism and fundamentalism. Richard Dawkins (compare chap. 2), who represents an aggressive atheism, and American representatives of creationism or intelligent design, which stand for aggressive anti-Darwinism, actually do the job for one another. How easy it is for the creationists to say, "Look how dreadful you become if you believe in Darwin!" How easy it is for Dawkins to say, "Look how hostile the Christians are to the sciences!" Both of them are equally wrong.

Opposition to the theory of evolution does in fact have very little to do with science and with God, particularly among the religious right in the US. It has all the more to do with conservative values. This can be illustrated by a statement following the shooting at Columbine High School at Littleton, Colorado, in 1999, which was repeated no less than three times (June 14, 16, 22) in the American Congress. This statement claimed that the causes of this violence should not be sought in great and easy availability of firearms in American society but rather in broken homes, daycare centers, TV and computer games, sterilization and contraceptives, abortions, and "because our school systems teach the children that they are nothing but glorified apes who have evolutionized out of some primordial soup of mud by teaching evolution as fact and by handing out condoms as if they were candy."

We make a mistake if we disregard this particular American context and exalt the conflict that is going on there into a universal conflict that might be characteristic of the relationship between science and faith in general. Nothing could be more wrong. The mainstream of Christian theology has no difficulties with the basic thinking of the theory of evolution.

Christianity is basically a science-affirming and a technology-friendly religion. This does not mean that there is no reason to initiate discussions on scientific theories and to ask critical questions about different technologies, for example about their long-term effects and what consequences they might have for "the little ones" in this world—those whom Jesus encourages us to take care of especially.

God, the Brain, and the Soul

Is God a figment of the imagination? The question about faith and the brain is interesting, but it is unfortunately often treated in a superficial, incomplete, and biased manner. Those who ask that question often seem to take for granted that experiences of God are flights of fancy that obstinately remain even though it seems certain that God only exists in our brains and nowhere else. But the question about God and our brains is too exciting and too important to be left to

BEYOND THE CARICATURES

those who start from the point of view that God is nothing other than a figment of our brains.

There is no doubt that God does exist in our brains. God is there just as fish, trees, thunderstorms, and hunger are. But, to begin with, the fact that these things exist in our thoughts says nothing at all about whether fish, trees, thunderstorms, and hunger only haunt our brains or whether they exist in external reality.

It is quite fascinating that we can come to grasp what it is that happens in our brains when we pray and have deep spiritual experiences. For example, it has turned out that when a meditating person reaches so deep into meditation that he or she experiences a sense of unity with the All, there is a strongly decreased activity in that part of the brain that helps us to orientate ourselves in space, which seems quite reasonable.

The ability to see that a specific activity—or inactivity—in the brain is linked to a certain kind of experience gives valuable information, but this knowledge does not give any complete explanation of our experiences or of our emotional life. If—expressed with a simplified analogy—we can identify a typical pattern of activity in the brain that emerges when we experience joy, this does not mean that joy is only a figment of the brain or that joy is meaningless. Brain research cannot explain away experiences and emotions in that way. It has however increased our awareness of the brain and the body as an integrated whole. It is not the case that the brain is some rational control center that governs an unintelligent body mass. We are unities in which the body, including the brain, is an active part in all relationships that we experience.

We do not know with any certainty why our brain has developed to include a capacity for religious experiences. Some theories seek the answer in more-or-less speculative explanations about why we have been programmed to assume supernatural agents all the time. This programming would in that case have been the beginning of all religion. But it would also be possible to build on the observation that human beings in various respects are the most social of all the animals that we know of—both in terms of dependence on social relationships and the ability to create them. The human need and will to relate and communicate seems insatiable. Is it an outflow of this basic sociality that human beings cannot refrain from endeavoring to engage even in a relationship with that which supersedes ordinary reality, with the transcendent or the holy? Is prayer a consequence of this? Could this social ability be one of the driving forces of religion?

Of course God "haunts" the brain. How would we otherwise be able to have any relationship to God? But saying that God haunts the brain does not imply that the divine reality is thus exhaustively described. I am convinced that it is greater than that. God is greater than my brain—and I also believe that God is greater than everybody's brains. To speak with the words of the Bible: "In him we live and move and have our being." According to Acts 17, the apostle Paul spoke those words when he addressed the people in the marketplace in Athens. He continued: "We ought not to think that the deity is like gold, or silver, or stone, an image formed by the art and imagination of mortals" (Acts 17:28–29). Today he might have said: "We ought not to think that the deity is like some neurons, like some brain activity that mortals could scan with their technological skills."

We can neither speak to or of God without making images of God. Some of our images of God are extremely sophisticated and artistic. But not even the most artistic images of God are God. They can however become icons that open windows toward the divine reality beyond. That is how the Eastern churches, the

Orthodox traditions, think about the icons that can be found in churches and in homes. And that is precisely how the icons on our computer screens work as well. A click and the reality beyond the icon opens up. The relationship to God does not work as automatically as that, but even our images of God can open up when we "click" on them with our longing. In a similar way, highly technological images of the activities of the brain can become windows into the divine reality that has attracted human beings ever since their evolutionary origin.

But what about the soul? It is not so very long ago that we spoke about how many souls belonged to a parish, or how many souls worshiped. Today such phrases sound strange—as if we were not always our bodies, or as if it is only the soul that matters when it comes to faith. The idea of the soul as some sort of natural core is of course deeply rooted, particularly in the cultures that consider that the cradle of their civilization stood in Greece—that is, in the entire Western sphere. The poetry of a hymn likens the soul to a butterfly: "Yesterday you were included in the pupa, today you happily broke out of your prison" (Current Swedish Hymnal from 1986, 304:3). At the moment that the body dies, the soul receives its longed-for freedom.

The immortal soul flies to heaven before the body is embedded in the earth.

From a theological perspective, the immortality of the soul is not at all self-evident. It is in fact quite a contentious question. Even so, the question, "Do you believe in an immortal soul?" is often included in investigations that want to measure the religiosity of people, as if the idea of the immortality of the soul was a trustworthy marker of (Christian) faith. The foremost theologian of the Bible on life and death, the apostle Paul, would hardly have ticked the "Yes" on this question. Nor would the prophets of the Old Testament. According to Paul and the prophets, we die when we die, without any part of us surviving.

On the one hand, human beings really die: there is no secret passage through which some part of humans might escape death. On the other hand, according to Paul, human beings die together with Jesus Christ to a life of resurrection (1 Corinthians 15). New life presupposes death. A life beyond death can only be received at the cost of death. And if that was the case for Jesus Christ, it will hardly be different for those who follow him, Paul reasons. The radical events that happened to Jesus seem to exclude any possibility that the soul might, so to speak, escape death by the back door.

GOD IS GREATER

For Paul, the hope of new life is based, not on any indwelling quality of humanity, but on God's promise and on God's power to create new life out of death.

When the media in the 1980s paid attention to Harvard Divinity School professor Krister Stendahl's (1921–2008), then bishop of Stockholm, rejection of the idea of the immortality of the soul, this caused something of a popular storm on the letters-to-the-editor pages. "We are already secularized, and now a bishop deprives us of the last little bit of faith we had left!" Stendahl rejected the idea of immortality for good theological reasons. He believed that it is far too great and at the same time far too small. It is far too great because it arrogantly glorifies the human being with individual immortality and claims to know more than is useful for us. At the same time it is far too small, far too egoistic, and far too concerned with one's own self, one's own family, or one's race. The great message of the New Testament, the advent of the reign of God, should not be sacrificed on the altar of human self-absorption. The main question is not what will happen to me, but what will happen to the struggle that God fights on behalf of God's creation.

Even from a scientific perspective, the concept of the soul is not altogether easy. The materialist-minded brain researcher might come up with the same statement as the materialist-minded astronaut: I was out there, and I did not find any God; I looked into the brain, and I did not find any soul. Such gross simplifications are easy to counter. But it is not so easy to find a way to speak about the soul that is theologically sound and that can be communicated in an age when brain research and cognitive science are making major progress.

We can distinguish between at least two ways of speaking about the soul. We can refer to the soul as a unit separated from the body, or even as the opposite of the body, but it is also possible to speak of the soul as an integral aspect of being human. For both theological and scientific reasons, the latter way is better. We also speak of the heart in a similar way: even though we have learned that it is a muscle that pumps blood, we still find it meaningful to say that someone is "of a good heart" or has "an open heart." And maybe if worse comes to worst, someone will get their "heart crushed," which in turn will probably make those who are close to that person extend "heartfelt sympathy." And unexpected signs of affection might "warm the cockles of the heart." It is quite possible to be aware that there is no empirically measurable soul that can be distinguished from the brain or consciousness and yet speak of the soul as something specific. When we speak of body and soul, or body and spirit, we do not refer to two separate substances but to two aspects of being a human being. Talk about the soul as an indispensable aspect of being human counteracts the reduction of human beings to their biological functions.

In area after area dualistic ways of describing human beings have been left behind in favor of more holistic and physical models. The soul is no longer the opposite of the body. Nor is it a distinctive unit with an existence, awareness, or ability to act of its own. It is rather a physiological quality of human nature. We can see it as an emerging quality that is decisive for our ability to relate to other people.

Many of the opposites that have been taken for granted for a long time have nowadays been questioned and abandoned. To those belong the contrast between freedom and conformity to law as well as the separation of humanity from the rest of creation. In this respect we focus more on continuity and differences of degrees, and we are less preoccupied by noting differences of essence. We no longer oppose the soul against the body but perceive it as one of the qualities that arises and develops in continuity with being a body and being a part of the rest of nature.

This change to our approach has practical significance in an age when environmental and climate issues are among the greatest challenges on our planet. A non-dualistic understanding is ecological in a deeper sense than the dualistic approaches that it has replaced.

In Praise of Wisdom

In a globalized world in which religion plays a major role for the majority of its citizens, theological analysis is needed in order to illuminate the processes that are seminal for the development of both science and technology. Science and technology have such fundamental significance for global life that we must consider them in a wider context. That must be a context that allows room for sociological and anthropological perspectives, and includes the various religious traditions as well as theological reflection.

I hope I have been able to show that we are right in not arguing in the way that the primatologist Vogel and the theologian Pannenberg did, who were both mentioned at the start of this chapter. Theology is not some irrelevant little balloon somewhere in the far distance. Nor is it a necessary, controlling authority for scientific research. However, theological issues and perceptions have always been present, and they still are in the air we all breathe—regardless of whether we consider science or theology our area of expertise, or whether we are more the so-called consumers of scientific and theological knowledge.

Irrespective of the discussions of language, hermeneutics, metaphors, and the public reception of science and theology, the presence of the major questions of our existence gives sufficient reason for the sciences and religion or theology, all of which are such culture-forming forces, to create opportunities for shared and mutual processes of learning.

Awe and wonder have always been a source of inspiration for both research and adoration. This common gushing spring encourages a life-affirming humility in face of what we do not yet know and reverence before that which is a mystery. Unlike a puzzle that loses its attraction when it has been solved, the genuine mystery grows deeper and deeper the more we become familiar with it. There is a wisdom that outshines our knowledge, a knowledge that at least in this world remains fragmentary.

The famous painting by Michelangelo (1475–1564) in the Sistine Chapel, in which the finger of God the creator touches the finger of Adam, has been endlessly popularized and travestied. What is rarely included in the presentations is God's left side. That too is exciting, because by God's left arm, God holds a woman, Wisdom. Without making any claim to offering the correct interpretation of Michelangelo's intentions, his famous painting becomes an illustration of what theologians have said in various ways: God is a relationship of love and not a scientific hypothesis. This relationship of love includes a love of wisdom. The thirst for wisdom holds us human beings together—in our scientific research with its technological applications, in our theological research with its confessional applications, in our philosophizing, in our deep longing for meaning, in our enormous anxiety in the face of what is imperfect and a failure, and in our intensive lust for what is good.

Therefore the prayer of King Solomon for wisdom, which probably originated in the last century before our common era, will end this chapter:

> May God grant me to speak with judgment,
> and to have thoughts worthy of what I have received;
> for he is the guide even of wisdom

and the corrector of the wise.
For both we and our words are in his hand,
as are all understanding and skill in crafts.
For it is he who gave me unerring knowledge of what exists,
to
know the structure of the world and the activity of the elements;
the beginning and end and middle of times,
the alternations of the solstices and the changes of the seasons,
the cycles of the year and the constellations of the stars,
the natures of animals and the tempers of wild animals,
the powers of spirits[a] and the thoughts of human beings,
the varieties of plants and the virtues of roots;
I learned both what is secret and what is manifest,
for wisdom, the fashioner of all things, taught me.

There is in her a spirit that is intelligent, holy,
unique, manifold, subtle,
mobile, clear, unpolluted,
distinct, invulnerable, loving the good, keen,
irresistible, beneficent, humane,
steadfast, sure, free from anxiety,
all-powerful, overseeing all,
and penetrating through all spirits
that are intelligent, pure, and altogether subtle.
For wisdom is more mobile than any motion;
because of her pureness she pervades and penetrates all things.
(Wis 7:15–22, 24)

4

Cosmic Passion History: In a Complex World Evil Has Several Roles

It was the fall of 2001, only a few weeks after I had started to teach at the Lutheran School of Theology at Chicago. But above all, it was only a few weeks after September 11, the event that overshadowed everything else at that time.

On a midweek day I was having lunch with a few students in the school's cafeteria. We were discussing the atmosphere in the country. The students criticized the official rhetoric that "they hate our freedom and our openness—and we will get them." To divide up the world into saints (us) and coward criminals (them) was not the right strategy for combating evil, they thought.

I told them what I had just read in some Swedish daily papers online: Some Swedes with a Somalian background had ended up on the US list of terrorists. Among other things, their financial assets had been frozen—as it seemed, mostly by mistake. They appeared to be innocent.

An hour or so later there was a knock at my office door. It was Mary, one of the students that I had shared the luncheon table with. She was studying to become a pastor. "What you told us leaves me no peace," she began. "I can't cope with the thought that the panic that prevails in my country affects innocent people somewhere far away in the world. It is not right." I agreed with Mary, but at the same time I quietly wondered what she thought she could do about that. "I have come to ask you to find the telephone number to the lawyer who is acting for those who have been affected. I want to contact the lawyer and ask how I could help." Mary made me think of her namesake, the mother of Jesus, and her Magnificat: "God has shown strength with his arm ... he has lifted up the lowly" (Luke 1:46-55). She got the telephone number.

Checking the *Swedish National Encyclopedia,* evil does not appear to be very important. There is no article on "evil" in the foremost reference book in Sweden. I do not know what the reason is—if the omission is based on a deliberate choice, or whether it just happened like that.

Maybe it is a result of the spirit of the age at the late twentieth century. Sweden has managed for over two hundred years to keep out of the evil that is spelled w-a-r, for example. Objectivity, security, rationality, and pragmatism have reigned for a long time at the political as well as at the personal level. The fruits are moderation and a love of cautiousness. Whatever feels safe and secure will win over anything that might be even better but feels more risky. This seems to be a successful recipe for keeping "the great evil" at a distance.

The picture is completed by skepticism toward such shared ideals that can become dangerous because they carry a seed of fanaticism. Attitudes that see values as expressions of subjective emotions are favored instead. Values belong primarily to the private sphere—that too is an expression of individualism. In the public arena the arguments are dressed up in the language of matter-of-factness as far as possible. "Work on the foundation of values" sounds more objective than "conversations about values." Objectivity appears to be a broader and firmer starting point than personal values, which might seem to rest on a narrower and less-stable foundation.

What is universal can be found in objectivity, while what is individual rests on more-or-less subjective values. Faith is often considered to belong to the latter. But the question is whether this division has not reached the end of the road.

In the words of cultural writer Håkan Boström: "During the era of the height of the Swedish Welfare State, objectivity was by and large uncontested. Progression had replaced religion and morals as the guide for life. But gradually faith in technology and in society has been replaced by what can best be described as narcissism."

The growth of material prosperity and the "technocratization" of politics have made the citizens turn inward, Boström believes. The focus of society has moved away from production to consumption. Behind this development, he sees glimpses of the philosophy of the Uppsala professor Axel Hägerström (1868–1939), whose thinking is usually denoted anti-idealist and value-nihilist, and whose motto was: "Besides, I believe that metaphysics should be destroyed." Boström writes: "Hägerström's utopia was a more rational society. But now, about a century later, it is an emotionally governed conformity that dominates society. . . . The fall of the ideals did not lead to the triumph of reason—but to docility and navel-gazing." There are therefore, according to Boström, good reasons to revise the heritage from Hägerström. "The fact is that even true individualists need something to fight for—something outside themselves."

Something to fight for is needed—maybe that is the reason why interest in value issues never expires. And there is also a need for something to fight against and hopefully to conquer: evil. In order to be efficient in that fight, a realistic description of what evil is, is needed—something that, unfortunately, the *Swedish National Encyclopedia* does not provide for us.

I cannot escape the thought that this silence might be an expression of the spirit of a time that would like to believe that most things are under control: deadly epidemics through hygiene and vaccination; poverty through social and political measures; superstition and stupidity through enlightenment and education; war through neutrality; conflicts through making sure that everyone has sufficient space and thinks more or less the same. At the end of the twentieth century we had acquired a kind of individualism that means large groups of the population do more or less the same thing but often one by one, on their own. The well-organized and well-oiled social machinery carries on. Some creaking and some operational glitches might occur, but there is a manual available for solving these problems. Among the primary methods are broad educational information campaigns. In such a world, evil appears almost as an anachronism—just as obsolete as the view that an illness, such as epilepsy, would be the result of demonic obsession. Evil is not perceived as a social reality but belongs to the mythological treasure house of history.

Whenever evil nevertheless presses in upon us, we lack both a language and appropriate ways to relate to it. Wherever the ideals have withered away and deep discussions of ideas and morals are mostly absent, the emotionally governed narcissism that Boström has described takes over. You can engage in Twitter storms rather than making an effort to analyze and understand the backgrounds. You can compete in making demands for condemnations of terrorism without engaging in doing something about its causes. You can transform forums for debate into places of intellectual execution and counteract shared action initiatives by polarization.

What is lacking in the *Swedish National Encyclopedia* can, not unexpectedly, be found in the liturgical tradition of the church. In the Church of Sweden Lectionary, the Third Sunday in Lent has the theme "The Fight against Evil."

Some lines from a sermon that I preached myself on that Sunday in 1986 can illustrate what I mean by the spirit of the time. I think it was a quite typical sermon, similar to many others in Sweden on that particular Sunday or in that week.

> Last week the theme of "evil" seemed very remote. It seemed far-fetched to speak of Jesus and evil. But because of what happened the night before Saturday, we have suddenly been touched by evil. For we were all touched by the murder of Olof Palme [Swedish Prime Minister, 1969–1976 and 1982–1986]. It was as if a wave of evil had swept through our entire country and surprised us all, the whole population, in our considerably great naivety. Consternation about what happened has shaken the people in our country, but it also created community between us. Days such as these strengthen us in our insight that we need one another, that we must stick together against evil. Maybe we even experience greater mutual understanding than what we manage to raise in everyday life. And at the same time we are aware of how powerless we are against evil.

One of the prayers on the Third Sunday in Lent reads: "God, you are our refuge when evil and powerlessness overwhelm us, we pray for wisdom, healing, courage and strength to fight in your name against evil, and to trust in your possibilities."

Deep experience and knowledge are hidden in these short lines. Evil overwhelms us; evil gives rise to feelings of powerlessness. Reactions can consist of blind, white-hot anger, aggression, resignation, or the play-dead reflex, which can help our survival but rarely much more than that. This prayer therefore speaks of a longing for wisdom rather than blind anger, for healing instead of aggression, for courage instead of cowardice, and for strength instead of weariness. And the prayer ends with a vision: we ask for faith in God's possibilities, for a world and a life beyond evil.

Can we get rid of evil? Can we eradicate evil? The answer is fairly obvious: no, but we can and we should fight against evil, and sometimes even conquer it.

On Earthquakes and Greediness

The issue of evil has often been approached by distinguishing between natural and moral evil. Natural evil includes natural catastrophes, such as the eruption of volcanoes, earthquakes, floods, and droughts—all of which affect people without their responsibility. Moral evil includes human, more or less artfully conceived, evil intentions and actions.

The catastrophic earthquake and the following tidal wave in Lisbon on the Feast of All Saints in 1755 have been perceived by many people as a typical example of natural evil. It gave rise to questions that were not unlike those that were aroused by the tsunami in December 2004 and by the earthquake catastrophe in Japan in March 2011, when among other things an atomic power plant was destroyed. Do we really live in the best of all worlds, as the philosopher and mathematician Gott-fried Wilhelm von Leibniz (1646–1716) claimed? Why do such horrible catastrophes occur if creation is good? Where is God in all this? As far as we can see, human activity had nothing to do with the earthquake itself that caused the tidal wave, but it has been claimed that human actions contributed to worsening its consequences. In connection with the tsunami, it became obvious that the devastation of mangrove forests close to the coastline and the unwise exploitation of coastal areas led to disastrous consequences. There are natural explanations to the fact that Japan is often hit by earthquakes and also by tsunamis. If and where nuclear power plants are built and how they are maintained is, however, a human responsibility. Similar arguments were put forward already in 1755. The philosopher Jean-Jacques Rousseau (1712–1778) believed, for example, that such major concentrations of populations as in Lisbon were unnatural.

To prove the degree of human responsibility for the consequences of natural catastrophes is complicated. Even so, this issue is more relevant than ever these days. Events that in the past occurred only because of the cycles of nature itself can nowadays show more-or-less clear traces of human influence and action. This applies, for example, to the changing patterns of precipitation and water flows, to the sources of water supply becoming salty, to the extension of deserts, and to the increased intensity of hurricanes.

The dividing line between natural and moral evil appeared much clearer in the past. In practice, the distinction between natural and moral evil is perhaps no longer of much help. In January and February 2010, severe earthquakes hit Haiti and Chile. Even though the latter was considerably stronger—so strong that it moved the axis of the globe—the number of casualties was lower and the damage lighter than in Haiti. The reason was not only differences in the density of population but above all the extent of poverty and the deficiencies in the infrastructure.

Even though the dividing line between natural and moral evil has in practice become much less obvious, there is still some reason to make a philosophical difference between natural and moral evil. It affects the way in which we can think and act against evil.

How Can We Relate to Natural Evil?

Why do earthquakes happen if creation is meant to be good? The traditional view that God created the world from nothing, *creatio ex nihilo*, has its proper place within Christian theology. It safeguards God's sovereignty by excluding the presence of any competing powers at the moment of creation. It also stresses the goodness of creation: if everything originates from the creating word of a good God, nothing can fall outside and become a ball for any evil power equal to God to play with. The perception of creation out of nothing aims to arouse trust in God who will in the end bring creation to a good and perfect completion.

However, there is also a weakness connected with the theology of *creatio ex nihilo.* It sharpens the theodicy problem, that is, the question of the existence of evil in a world that has been created by a good God. The God who creates from nothing once and for all will inevitably become the object of the eternal suspicion that might compare God to the famous architect Frank Lloyd Wright (1867–1959): he was able to create enormously beautiful buildings, but he was less successful as an engineer. In spite of the beauty, some people died from pneumonia in his houses because it was not possible to create a sound indoor climate there. Should not God, known and loved as the creator of heaven and earth, be able to do better than that?

Some contemporary theologians have wondered whether the idea of creation from chaos might be closer to the diversity of biblical texts, and even closer to nature as we understand it, than the idea of *creatio ex nihilo*. From a mythological perspective, chaos has often been understood as evil. There is the slaughter of a primeval chaos beast as a presupposition for the creation of cosmos, as in the story of Tiamat in the Babylonian epic of creation, the *Enuma Elish*.

The process theologian Catherine Keller (b. 1953) has argued in favor of an interpretation that breaks away from the one-sided identification of chaos as evil and of order as goodness. She calls the view of *creatio ex nihilo* "tehomophobic"—from the Greek *phobia*, "fear," and the Hebrew *tehom*, "the depth," the chaos waters, the waters over which the divine wind swept according to the first (but not the oldest) creation story of the Bible (Gen 1:2). According to Keller, the idea of *creatio ex nihilo* does more damage than good because it demonizes *tehom* by letting it appear as only evil. Thus we lose sight of its creative potential. Why would order automatically be good and disorder automatically evil?

Taking this thought as the starting point, Keller has highlighted the more *tehom*-friendly passages that can also be found in the creation stories in the Bible, and whose strength we have missed when we have considered all creation motifs only in the light of creation out of nothing. The water and the earth bring forth things (Gen 1:20–24)—they are cocreators rather than mere elements in a linear process. God rejoices in the play of Leviathan, the chaos animal in Psalm 104:26. In the Wisdom literature of the Bible, the tension between order and disorder is also less prominent.

Things happen to our worldview if chaos is not seen as an expression of pure evil but first and foremost as a playground for possibilities. Keller speaks of the danger of diminishing the role of chaos in creation. The fear of chaos can lead to a preference for hierarchic and oppressive structures that are often damaging to natural and social environments. Keller therefore suggests that we should take a pause for a while from the *creatio ex nihilo* scheme and work with the idea of a *creatio ex profundis*—a creation from the depths of God's nature, which is then perceived as a multidimensional continuum of possible relationships.

To allow this deep space of possibilities to dry up would be fatal—as fatal as draining the earth's aquifers. The attempts to force the wildness and unpredictability of nature into a linear scheme of order have often led to disastrous consequences for the environment. They have hit back at humanity and damaged ecological systems. But just as disastrous as this exploitation, undertaken in the name of order, has turned out to be, so it might of course also be disastrous to romanticize disorder. When it comes to our attitude toward creation, it has often been difficult to keep firmly on the road and all the easier to slide off into the ditches.

Bacon's early seventeenth-century view of nature as a wild woman who should be tamed and be stripped of its treasures (see chap. 3) led down into the ditch of grave exploitation. A view of nature that is merely fascinated by fine-tuned balance and closes its eyes to the struggle for survival that is continuously raging in nature will end up in the ditch of romanticism. Neither of these alternatives offers a possible road ahead. It cannot be a matter of either order or chaos. It is rather about interplay between chaos and order, and about opening our eyes to the risky characteristics of nature and creation. Creating always implies taking risks, evidently also for the Creator with a capital C.

In our day and age, the knowledge that research into complexity has generated is relevant for the question about natural evil. In an exciting way, it provides support for the theological thinking I have just mentioned. The Danish physicist Per Bak (1948–2002) has coined the phrase "self-organized criticality." It can be used, for example, to describe the maximal incline of a growing pile of sand. The moment when the next grain of sand will trigger an avalanche rather than lying down almost unnoticed next to the other grains can never be predicted. This observation seems to confirm catastrophism, that is, the opposite of the philosophy that claims that development always takes place gradually and continually. Catastrophes occur by necessity when complex systems develop, and they are caused by very minor events.

This thought has its correspondence in apocalypticism, in the portrayal of the enormous catastrophes that at the end of time, it is believed, will precede and accompany the end of the world. Nowadays apocalypticism seems to be more appreciated by filmmakers than by theologians. Its more well-behaved cousin, eschatology (from the Greek *ta eschata*: "the ultimate things," which can be interpreted existentially as well as chronologically), has for a long time been far more popular than this ungovernable *enfant terrible*. However, maybe it is time to reconsider the theological evaluation of apocalypticism, particularly in areas where natural evil and moral evil reinforce one another, which we can clearly observe with regard to the issues of the climate and the environment. When climate researchers speak of "tipping points," threshold events that lead to major and irreversible changes, it is certainly about a scenario of apocalyptic scale.

I believe that in a way, research can help us tackle the unsolved and, as it seems, unsolvable theodicy problem. In nature, new and complex patterns are continually developing. They seem to emerge more or less as surprises in the interplay between various factors. Researchers speak of "emergence"—a process whose unpredictable development only appears to us afterward. Emergence produces "something more from nothing but," as the biologist Ursula Goodenough (b.

1943) and the anthropologist Terrence Deacon have expressed it. In nature, the emergence of this complexity seems to come at a price: it requires not only order and continuity but also disorder and new impetus.

In other words: criticality and catastrophes have a place in nature, just as continuity and stability. Creativity can be understood as a continual striving toward further development, not least during phases of crisis and upheaval. Thus natural evil is placed in a context of meaning even though that does not imply that we experience it as meaningful. There is reason to assume that what we experience as natural evil has a significant role to play in the continued development of nature—or, theologically speaking, in God's continuously ongoing work of creation.

I am not saying this in order to trivialize suffering or evil. Nor do I believe that it is a satisfactory explanation of the extent of evil. Suffering that is understood within the framework of the development of nature does not therefore cease to be suffering.

From a Christian point of view, we can approach the issue of natural evil and its cosmic scope from the perspective of the theology of the cross. We have no final answers as to why the history of evolution is marked by so many events that, according to our way of looking at them, are catastrophes that have caused suffering of enormous proportions. Of course we can get carried away by the fine-tuning and the sense of purpose in what might appear as a cosmic symphony. But this exalted sentiment does not make us forget the aspects of suffering and the character of evolution as passion history.

When we interpret the history of the universe in that way, as a cosmic passion history, something fascinating occurs: the cross, the most exclusive symbol of Christianity, simultaneously gains radically inclusive significance. It provides an interpretation of our entire existence as we can perceive it with the best knowledge available to us. This thought has been masterfully and simply expressed by the Swedish pastor and poet Anders Frostenson in his hymn for Lent (Swedish Hymnal 438): "You, who in the midst of the universe have placed the cross on which you give yourself, have given us this time of Lent for healing, light and life." The place of the cross in the midst of the universe implies that all work of creation is a gift of self, that it means taking a risk, even for the creator. And it means that suffering as well as the victory of life belongs to the very nature of existence. The cross has a universal meaning.

In that sense the Christian church does not have an exclusive right to the cross—its embrace is wider than that. The Christian faith is carried along by an unyielding hope precisely because it trusts that the cosmic passion history is crossed through and translucently illuminated by an even greater and more passionate passion, that is, by God's love for the world (John 3:16). It is not possible to relate to evil only by the tools of logic. Logic and passion are not mutually exclusive.

Since we lack final answers, linguistic expressions are all the more important. Not being able to find any emotional or intellectual expressions of suffering makes the evil worse. That is the reason why lament is and must continue to be a significant part of religious language and religious rites. A liturgy that only sings "Glory to God in the highest" without leaving room for the cries of "Lord, have mercy" is not credible. In all their untidy immediacy, the book of Lamentations and other songs and psalms of lament in the Bible have a self-evident place in the liturgy of worship as well as in our daily life. Between the jubilant *Gloria* and the destitute *Kyrie*, there is rainbow of different languages of prayer.

What Can We Say about Moral Evil?

We cannot ever root out natural evil, but we can ask ourselves critically if our own actions make it worse and how we can alleviate its consequences.

"The love of money is a root of all kinds of evil," 1 Timothy affirms (6:10). Bearing in mind the financial crisis in the first decade of the twenty-first century, it is easy to agree. The crisis that became a fact in 2008 revealed a degree of human greediness that surpassed most things. It is alarming that the cries for a radically new orientation in economic thinking and in financial practice did not have any major effect. In many places things fairly immediately returned to "business as usual." Twice as much money as was needed in order to fulfill the UN millennium goal to cut in half the poverty of the world was produced without too much trouble in order to save the banks. What does this say about how evil is perceived, and about what the collective readiness to fight evil looks like? What do we need to know in order to take up the fight against evil in an effective manner? The word of God to Cain is ringing in my ears: "If you do not do well, sin is lurking at the door; its desire is for you, but you must master it" (Gen 4:7). For Cain, things did not go well. It is possible to

COSMIC PASSION HISTORY

be more successful. Knowledge of how evil functions is important. But more is needed.

Moral evil can of course be irrational, but very often it is also frighteningly rational. Reason is neither the opposite of evil nor the sole best weapon against it. Evil is far from always the same as irrationality or emotions that have gone wrong or overboard. Evil can be governed by reason and very systematic. Just think of the evil that appeared under the title "the final solution to the Jewish problem"—the formulation itself says a great deal about the rationality of the Holocaust machinery, a machinery that was kept going by ordinary people. During the Cold War as well as during the war against terrorism since 2001, science was mobilized in order to develop effective methods of torture as well as other things.

When evil is defined as an attack on reason—without any connection to the whole register of emotional tones—the fight against evil easily becomes a matter of bargaining with fear as the primary capital. That was by and large what we saw happening in the United States after September 11, 2001. The attack, which was defined as an attack on the rationality of the American ideal of freedom, paved the way for the successful but fateful rhetoric, for which the prime fuel was fear: the axis of evil, the war against terrorism, and George W. Bush's self-assumed messianic responsibility to liberate the world from evil. "My responsibility in the face of history is to liberate the world from evil" is precisely how the president expressed himself at the National Prayer and Memorial Service in the Washington National Cathedral on September 14, 2001. In contrast, here are the words of a Messiah who expressed himself far more modestly when he prayed for his friends: "I am not asking you to take them out of the world, but I ask you to protect them from the evil one" (John 17:15).

To play reason and emotions against one another in the face of evil makes us easy prey to absurdities. According to an investigation, flight passengers are prepared to pay considerably more for an additional insurance policy that is valid in case of death as a consequence of terrorism than compared to a general insurance that is valid in case of death in general. The word *terrorism* obviously triggers an almost uncontrollable anxiety that puts most of people's logical thinking aside, such as the ability to make logical considerations of probability, for example.

Evil must be understood within the field of tension between reason and emotions, which is so difficult to penetrate. Neither pure reason nor naked emotions are enough to describe evil, and even less sufficient for dealing with it and fighting it. Moral evil is both rational and irrational at the same time. Therefore it cannot be fought by reason alone, nor only at the emotional level. The financial crisis is a clear example of this mixture. It was the result of a failed ethical leadership, not only a failure of a rational system of rules and regulations. This opens up a frightening perspective: within the financial world, things were done that hardly anyone would have become involved in at the individual level, since they would then have appeared as clearly dishonest. Nevertheless that same behavior seems to have been acceptable in the field of business. That is not rational. And markets do not function in a rational manner either but rather according to chaos theory, according to which very minor factors might lead to enormous consequences. Nor is the shortsightedness that drives the market at quarter speed very rational in the long run.

An adequate way of relating to moral evil requires a holistic view of reason and emotions. Modern brain research has shown that the separation of reason and emotions is a construction that finds no support in the way in which our biology functions. In a well-functioning brain, rational and emotional processes are integrated. This integration must be taken into consideration when we seek to work out how best to relate to evil. Logic and passion belong together. Not only basic knowledge is required. We also need knowledge of the abyss.

And Then a Quarter of Spirituality

Besides reason and emotions, the fight against evil is also about spirituality in the sense of what drives us most deeply. It is not possible to consider the issue of evil in any way that is even approximately exhaustive without involving the religious traditions. Religion can be used or abused, just like anything else. In Swedish society we have been preoccupied by the negative sides of religion to such a degree that religion is sometimes seen as a problem rather than as a positive societal force. That is quite a paradox, since Sweden has experienced relatively little of the negative sides of religion compared to many other places in the world—and on the contrary quite a lot of its community-creating force: the strong commitment to education, medical, and social care is rooted in the practice of Christianity.

"Religion is experienced as a danger to society," the then–Discrimination Ombudsman (DO) Katri Linna said in an interview in 2009. "There is increasing questioning of the role of religion in people's everyday lives; about what conviction means and about how religion is practiced," she said in the interview, in which she noted that discrimination because of religion has been the area in which she has found it most difficult to create a dialogue. "People experience religion as a phenomenon that presents a danger to society—even in more upmarket circles there is a questioning which is very open and obvious." An idea or a conviction easily attracts the stamp of fanaticism. In fact, she said, "There is a kind of 'secularist fanaticism' in Sweden . . . people cannot understand that religion is important for other people. . . . This religious illiteracy makes Swedes believe that religion is something that an individual can choose to add to his or her life or choose not to engage in at all without any difficulty." Even though most DO matters on religious discrimination at that time were about non-Christian religions, Linna stressed that it was also about Christianity: "One is not allowed to express a strong faith, nor to let the children participate in religious activities, since that can be perceived as indoctrination. . . . It is not easy to be a practicing believer in Sweden, regardless of which religion." Against that background it is not surprising that in 2015 the Swedish National Council for Crime Prevention reported the highest level of hate crimes statistics so far. The greatest increase was in Christophobic hate crimes, but Islamophobic and anti-Semitic hate crimes also showed a noticeable increase among the police reports.

The difficulty in finding a balanced view of faith and religion is linked to the failing ability to find good ways of relating to evil. In December 2009 I participated together with an interfaith delegation from Sweden in the Parliament of the World Religions in Melbourne, Australia. Experiences from that part of the world made an obvious contrast to the Swedish reality that the DO was painting in the interview quoted above. Among the thousands of participants, and in the just over six hundred seminars that were offered, there was an almost stunning diversity. A theme that recurred again and again was the ability of religion to contribute to the good in the world and to counteract evil. It might concern such different issues as global financial ethics, the fight against corruption, the question of a secure supply of water and food, environment and climate, education, women's rights, and the fight against HIV.

A lesser-known aspect of the work of this Parliament consisted of an unexpected visit. Three high-ranking officials from the Obama administration came to Melbourne in order to meet leaders of different religions. According to the media reports, they wanted to gain knowledge of interfaith dialogue and to engage in conversations about the role of religion in finding good solutions in international politics. People might take diverse views on these conversations, but there is in fact a difference between being blind to the significance of religion and seeing religion as part of good solutions.

The latter alternative has, for example, been chosen by the police in the city of Melbourne and in the state of Victoria. There the police have a multireligious council whose task it is to work for collaboration with the faith communities. The program declaration says that the Victoria Police Multi-Faith Council originated in response to the increasing roles of the faiths in society. The starting point was that there is a common responsibility among all faith communities to create and maintain a well-functioning society. In that context, the Inter-Faith Council has a role. "Here we have many languages, many cultures and many faith traditions," the chair of the Council told us when we visited, "but we are *one* Melbourne."

Would it really be a good idea to cut off the streams of moral orientation that emanate from the traditions of the world religions? Is it a good idea to amputate ourselves from the Ten Commandments, the double commandment to love (which is in fact triple: love of God, neighbor, and oneself), the Golden Rule with its virtually universal character, and the challenging ideals of the Sermon on the Mount? Why do people in some places choose the view that democracy works best when existential and religious views are relegated to the strictly private sphere and discussions about values are kept as neutral as possible, whereas people in other places believe that religious and cultural diversity is a richness that can contribute to a flourishing democratic society?

The concept of value neutrality lost its epistemological innocence long ago. Value neutrality is no virtue, hardly even a possibility. A critical discussion of values is, however, both a virtue and a necessity. It is better to highlight particular starting points clearly than to refer to some universal consensus that rarely exists. There is often an overlapping consensus that makes it possible to collaborate across boundaries in some aspects in spite of the remaining differences in other areas.

I wonder if it might be time to recover the word *ideology*, which has come to arouse mostly negative associations. It evokes thoughts of a compulsory system of more or less nonscientific convictions, which suffocates and blinds people, renders an open and factual discussion more difficult, and prevents serious appropriation of knowledge. It can be like that. But it does not have to be like that. A positive meaning of the word *ideology* could be a well-thought-out and existentially well-founded set of ideas that can offer guidance while they are at the same time constantly being tested, both in theory and in practice. Nobody wants to be without ideas, while we do realize that not all ideas are good ones. Ideas do not exclude logic—constant ideologic testing is needed.

It is not the case that an affluent society automatically produces good people who can tackle the evil in the world in an exemplary manner. Moral nurture and self-discipline will remain a task as long as there are people—even though concepts such as the formation of character today tastes like nineteenth-century moralism.

It was at a seminar in Melbourne that I heard the dean of one of the most famous business schools in the United States complain, "My students are more eager to earn than to learn!" They would rather earn money than gain knowledge. A better ethics than the one that is described in this phrase does not come for free!

Precisely these efforts to find new financial models are among the primary challenges of our time in the fight against evil. Since the early seventeenth century, the economy has been driven by and based on colonialism. During the twentieth century, competition became its major driving force. In the twenty-first century, we are facing the task of achieving a humanization of the economy. If it was only short-term profit that applied some fifteen years ago, there is today greater attention paid to other parameters as well. Besides profit, sustainability also counts as well as the social consequences of financial activities. A sustainable market economy must be interested in ethically defensible profits, social well-being, and protection of the environment.

Some years ago, at an international high-level conference, a working group consisting of leaders from different parts of the world and different sections of society, such as companies, banks, research institutes, and voluntary organizations, was charged with producing a curriculum for training future CEOs to be able to run companies that will make this new economy a reality. The group concluded that a good curriculum must consist of four parts: a quarter economics, a quarter political reality, a quarter social responsibility, and a quarter spirituality. Here the spiritual sources of the religious traditions of the world were considered inevitable for the leadership that the world needs today.

An objection is voiced immediately: Could you not have good morality without religion? Would that not in fact be even nobler? The answer to the first question is, Yes, of course. But it would be very hard to show that it would be nobler. The argument that is usually put forward in this context is that the nonbeliever who does the good would be nobler than someone who does the good because of their faith, since the believer could be motivated either by the hope of a heavenly reward or by the fear of divine punishment. They would thus not do the good for its own sake, or for the sake of another human being, but in fact mostly for their own sake. However, it is surely the case that the personal satisfaction, regardless of any personal faith, in having resisted evil and having done something good is a positive driving force. If nothing else, it has positive health effects. Especially in Lutheran spirituality, it has been emphasized again and again that it is pointless to do good in order to collect points for heavenly rewards. Doing good is an outflow of the joy, gratitude, and love that is awakened by God's grace, forgiveness, and love. The moral driving force is found in the experience of being free to do the good. It can be experienced by the believer as an inner obligation ("The love of Christ urges us on," Paul says, for example, in 2 Cor 5:14) although not as a threat of reprisals.

Secular ethics is often influenced by those streams of religious ideology that it rejects. At a closer look, the similarities between them are greater than the differences. Secularity and religiosity are intertwined in some kind of common destiny—and from there spring the sometimes-aggressive tensions between them.

The Good Example and the Good Story

The fight against evil requires more than philosophical principles. It also needs the good example and the good story. One way to deal with evil, which has aroused both admiration and criticism, is the work of the Truth and Reconciliation Commission in South Africa after the fall of the apartheid regime. It has created a model as a deliberately chosen alternative to the methods used at the Nürnberg Trials following the Second World War. Nevertheless, it has been criticized for not going all the way—the whole truth could not be brought out, and it could not bring healing to the entire nation. The conflict between justice and forgiveness has no final solution in this world. But no doubt, the South African Truth and Reconciliation Commission did start many healing processes.

It is thought provoking that in Swedish, we often content ourselves to speak of the Truth Commission. The full name is in fact the Truth and Reconciliation Commission. Truth certainly creates freedom (John 8:32), but the fight against evil and victory over evil also require forgiveness and reconciliation.

Early on during my time as a bishop I visited a youth custody center in the diocese. "We are grateful to have access to a priest here," the director said. "Because when it does happen that some of our guys"—it was mostly boys there—"do come so far that they really understand the severity of what they have done, such as having killed another human being, then there is usually a need for something else besides the care that we can offer. Then forgiveness and reconciliation are needed."

In his book *No Future without Forgiveness* (1999), the chair of the Truth and Reconciliation Commission, Archbishop Emeritus Desmond Tutu, describes his initial surprise that President Nelson Mandela had appointed a theologian rather than a lawyer as the chair. His explanation is that the president must have thought that our work would basically be spiritual. *Forgiveness*, *confession*, *reconciliation*, and *atonement* surely are not very common terms in politics. Tutu writes that very few people opposed the obvious spiritual character of the work of the Commission. Even a Hindu colleague on the Commission insisted that the chair should wear his official episcopal garb. There was the experience that sometimes the language of prayer and lighted candles were needed as part of the work. "As I grow older, I have been joyfully surprised at the relevance of theology," Tutu says with his typical sense of humor. He highlights some central thoughts in Christian anthropology: to recognize one's responsibility for the evil deeds that have been committed and to resist the temptation to blame someone else, to resist demonizing the perpetrator, to distinguish between the offense and the offender, and to hold on to the hope that penitence and change are possible.

Tutu frequently speaks of *ubuntu*. This word is hard to translate. *Ubuntu* is about realizing the radical intertwining of everything. The humanity of the perpetrator is intertwined with that of the victim. Through the evil deed, both of them lose their humanity. *Ubuntu* means that a human being is a human being through other human beings. Personhood is not constituted by any Cartesian concentration on the core of the individual person in a *cogito ergo sum* ("I think, therefore I exist") but because I can say, "I belong, I participate, I exist." The Cartesian view incites critical thinking, individualism, and maybe even moral courage.

Sometimes this view would need a boost of *ubuntu* in order to counteract those aspects of individualism that damage the well-being of the community. *Ubuntu* stresses that it is the community that constitutes the ego. If this becomes too strong, maybe some Cartesian thinking might be needed in order to facilitate the kind of dissent that the community also needs in order to develop.

Theology, Tutu says, helped us in the Truth and Reconciliation Commission to see our universe as a moral universe in which both good and evil are real and matter. This led him to formulate the following creed: "For us who are Christians, the death and resurrection of Jesus Christ is proof that positive love is stronger than hate, that life is stronger than death, that light is stronger than darkness, that laughter and joy, and compassion and gentleness and truth, all these are so much stronger than their ghastly counterparts."

While the fight was still going on, he used to say: "This is a moral universe—the defenders of apartheid have already lost." And, he also said, forgiveness is in fact the best form of serving one's own interest since anger, grudge-bearing, bitterness, and vindictiveness corrode the social community that strengthens everyone's humanity and personality.

In the postscript to *No Future without Forgiveness*, Tutu reflects on how costly the work of the Truth and Reconciliation Commission has been for those who have participated in it—not measured in money but in terms of psychological symptoms such as stress, suffering, and breakdown. Maybe we were more like vacuum cleaners than dishwashers, he says: the dirt was not washed away but collected inside us. However, maybe it was only as "wounded healers" that we were actually able to contribute to reconciliation.

Whichever way we look at it, our way of approaching evil has to do with our faith. That connection can inspire people to heroic deeds, but it can also lead to the deepest failures in life. Faith can mislead, but it can also guide us in the right way—to the most remarkable resistance to evil. Whenever faith makes forgiveness possible, the most improbable can happen. Forgiveness can change an entire community, and it changes ourselves as well. In their book *Made for Goodness: And Why This Makes All the Difference* (2010), Desmond Tutu and his daughter Mpho Tutu put it like this: "When we forgive, we reclaim the power to create. We can create a new relationship with the person who has injured us. We can create a new story of ourselves. When we find the strength to forgive, we are no longer victims. We are survivors." Those two have later deepened these thoughts in their book *The Book of Forgiving—the Fourfold Path for Healing Ourselves and Our World* (2014).

Do I believe that faith solves every problem? Absolutely not. Do I believe that faith is a force that is needed in the fight against evil? Yes, absolutely.

A Fall into Sin, or a Leap into Awareness?

Martin Luther (1483–1546) was a person who had one foot in the Middle Ages, while with the other foot he was on his way into the modern era. The medieval view of the world appears here and there in Luther's dynamic view of human beings and their salvation. For him, there is a continual struggle about humanity between God and the devil. This struggle about every human being is something that he experienced in tangible ways. It was real, and it was dramatic. "Man between God and the Devil" was the subtitle that Heiko Oberman, one of the major Luther scholars of the twentieth century, chose for his presentation of Luther and his theology.

Latter-day Lutheranism has had a tendency to weed out these dramatic features. This demythologization has had its price: the dynamic process has been reduced to a dogmatic snapshot. And there has been a preference for exposing that image in black and white: humanity is either angelic or beastly, either Madonna or whore, either saved or damned. The empty space between these two extremes has been filled out by sin, a concept to which modern people find it increasingly difficult to relate.

However, the dynamic perspective did not disappear altogether. It had an exciting renaissance with Søren Kierkegaard (1813–1855) through the interpretation of the fall into sin that he offers in his book *The Concept of*

Anxiety. There the drama is back. Compared to Luther, there is, however, quite a significant difference. The battle about humanity is now no longer fought outside human beings, between God and the devil, but within human beings themselves. In that way *The Concept of Anxiety* provides a psychologizing theological interpretation that fits both the era of existentialism and that of late modernity.

I have been inspired by Kierkegaard's view that the story about the fall into sin (Genesis 3) must be read as a story of the awakening of freedom and the spirit. Kierkegaard starts from the assumption that the deep mystery of innocence is at the same time also anxiety. Innocence and lack of knowledge belong to a state of dreaming, which precedes awareness. As long as the spirit rests in this state of dreaming, freedom remains unrealized. Anxiety is the reality of freedom as a possibility of the possible, as Kierkegaard put it. This compressed sentence contains the existential drama in which humanity lives between good and evil. The realization of freedom as a possibility of what is possible cannot take place without anxiety. This is what Kierkegaard wrote: "Anxiety may be compared with dizziness . . . anxiety is the dizziness of freedom, which emerges when . . . freedom looks into its own possibility, laying hold of finiteness to support itself. Freedom succumbs to this dizziness. . . . In that very moment everything is changed, and freedom, when it again rises, sees that it is guilty. Between these two moments lies the leap which no science . . . has explained."

When we look down into the bottomless abyss of possibilities of freedom, we grab hold of finality in order not to lose our footing. We do so at the cost of perfect freedom. When our dizziness has subsided, we become aware of our bondage to the finite, and our innocence and unawareness are gone. We have become aware of the life of the spirit and of our own subjectivity. Therefore, anyone who has become familiar with anxiety in the right way has learned the greatest knowledge of all, Kierkegaard tells us. In order for human beings to become humans, they need this knowledge of the abyss.

Rather than a fall into sin, it is in fact more of a leap in which the life of the spirit and the possibilities of freedom are awakened at the price of the reality of sin and guilt. The story of the fall into sin is about the birth of insight, freedom, and the awareness of time. This birth is the precondition for us to be able to relate to evil outside ourselves, while at the same time it also opens our eyes to the possibilities of evil that dwell within each one of us.

Adam's and Eve's fall into sin is historical in the sense that it happens in the life of every Adam and Eve. In spite of its tragedy, and even more because of this tragedy, it is a leap in our development rather than a fall. This view presupposes an understanding of creation that corresponds to what I discussed before in this chapter with reference to Catherine Keller. It implies a greater valuation of possibility (freedom) in relation to reality (the finite) without thereby romanticizing away the risks. It is still anxiety and the experience of sin that we are talking about.

The concept of sin has been defined in various ways. Sometimes primarily as disobedience or as an offense against a commandment or a law, sometimes primarily as pride (*hubris*), sometimes as being turned in toward oneself (Luther), sometimes by the Greek athletic term *hamartia* as missing the goal. Sometimes the Germanic etymology of the word *sin* as separation has been chosen as the starting point, and sin has been defined as that which destroys our communion with God, with our fellow human beings, and with the entire creation as well as our relationship to ourselves. It is only natural that definitions should vary somewhat through time and space. An emancipated society finds it more difficult than an authoritarian society to define sin as disobedience. People who live with oppression and discrimination are not helped by *hubris* as the primary definition of sin, since in that context sin would rather imply a lack of pride.

The term *original* (hereditary) sin is nowadays seen as a problem, not least because it obscures its own opposite, "original (hereditary) goodness." Nevertheless, the phenomenon that this phrase denotes, that is, the deep ambiguity that is embedded at the very core of everything human, is universally human.

The concept of original (hereditary) sin itself is loaded with some misunderstandings. Ever since the days of the church father Augustine (354–430), it has been linked to the idea that sin is transmitted biologically from generation to generation through conception. This has in turn complicated the relationship to sexuality and its expressions. Since original sin has nothing to do with biological reproduction, the suitability of the concept as such can be questioned. The term itself is not indispensable and can be replaced. But the reality that this concept seeks to capture cannot be set aside, as also Kierkegaard has proved.

The English term *original sin*—primeval sin or, in the

existential sense, the basic sin—captures the matter somewhat better. We need to be able to describe how sin, the basic state in which every human being ends up when he or she, through "the leap of sin," becomes aware of his or her actions and his or her responsibility, expresses itself in various sins. We need descriptions that do justice to the drama that is played out between our bondage to sin, on the one hand, and our freedom and our moral responsibility, on the other hand. This deep ambiguity in everything human makes the boundaries between good and evil less unambiguous than we would wish.

Paul's analysis of this ambiguity in Romans 7 is as sharp as a knife. The inner struggle and agony that I have because I do not do the good that I want to do, and because I do the evil that I do not want to do, is not a luxury problem. We have a modern follower of Romans 7 in the book *Täter: Wie aus ganz normalen Menschen Massenmörder werden* [*Perpetrators: How Entirely Normal People Become Mass Murderers*] by Harald Welzer (2005). According to Welzer's analysis, everyone seems to be capable of the worst if only three conditions are fulfilled. If we get stuck sufficiently deeply in "us-and-them" thinking in which "they" cease to be our fellow human beings, if the limits of what is permitted are gradually stretched, and if a solidarity is created around the necessity of evil actions, just about anything can happen. Even so, and at the same time, it is also true that we have the opportunity to resist evil passionately, to work on ourselves and with one another to create a culture that cultivates life.

A life in which people live wholeheartedly in the consequences of the leap of sin is a world of possibilities and passions. Its description could be taken from the *Diapsalmata* in Kierkegaard's *Either/Or*: "Let others complain that our age is evil; my complaint is that it is paltry. For it is without passion. . . . That's why my soul always reverts to the Old Testament and to Shakespeare. . . . There people hate, people love, people murder their enemy and curse his descendants through all generations, there people sin." Better to live an extreme life than a life that suffocates in mediocrity, Kierkegaard seems to think. Better the depth of sins and passions than a narrowminded, rigid life! Whoever has not tasted the necessity and gift of forgiveness has not lived life. The worst thing the ego in the *Diapsalmata* knows is the loss of the gift of opportunity: "Were I to wish for anything I would not wish for wealth or power, but for the passion of the possible, that eye which everywhere, ever young, ever burning, sees possibility." Consequently, it is boredom and rigidity that we should fear more than the possibility of sin. It is better to take the risk that things might go wrong than to refrain from the opportunity to do something because of a fear that it might go wrong.

An expert on Kierkegaard would surely object here that my tribute to opportunity as the signature of freedom has missed the fact that the philosophy in the *Diapsalmata* belongs to what Kierkegaard has called the aesthetic stage of life. According to Kierkegaard, the aesthetic stage must be followed by the ethical. It is not the case that the aesthetic stage would in itself be bad or evil, but it has a disastrous deficiency: it does not understand the deep importance of making a choice. An ethical person is not primarily a person who strives to make the *right* choice between right and wrong. The ethical person is the one who chooses the *choice.*

To Be Set Free to Do Good

The ethical person, Kierkegaard thinks, can even choose despair if that is what is required in order to confront the abyss of existence in such a way that freedom is born. The ability and the will to engage ethically with tragedy are characteristic of the person who has become familiar with anxiety in the right way. This ability exposes even the paradoxical fact that taking care of the opportunity—creativity—is often accompanied by restlessness and anxiety. Creative people often live with inner tensions and far from the ideal of a life in harmony, far from what the book covers of feel-good literature suggest. Even in that sense, the words of Kierkegaard prove to be true: "Whoever has learned to be anxious in the right way has learned the ultimate." And the right way is certainly not suicidal anxiety.

Kierkegaard understood how to put words on the paradoxes of life. He did not always do so in ways that seem to be right and adequate today, but he did it thoughtfully and provocatively. He showed that to accept that existence is deeply ambivalent is not the same as saying goodbye to reason. The fact that the paradox surmounts sheer reason does not necessarily make it the opposite of reason. There is in fact a relationship between what is rational and what is more than rational. In that relationship human creative capacity is set free.

Faith lives in and with this relationship between the rational and the more-than-rational. Christian life is not about having faith against reason but having faith with reason, and sometimes beyond reason. When we have taken in what happens in "the leap of sin" we can, while keeping reason intact, come to grips with the inevitable choices in life. We know that we will all incur guilt. We become guilty. The acute situations that force us to make decisive choices might include unique opportunities for growth and happiness while they can also lead to guilt and unhappiness. This is our tragedy. It cries out for the cross—the cross "in the midst of the universe" that also stands in the midst of our own, very personal lives. There too Jesus gives himself to bring healing and light and life. In the power of the cross, the way of guilt becomes a way to liberation. The cross shows us the way through death to life. Good Friday is followed by Easter morning.

This insight led Luther to make the unexpected and rather shocking exhortation: *Pecca fortiter*—"Sin boldly!" Not because of carelessness, but because of faith. Faith does not turn away from the tragedy that is a consequence of the cosmic passion history and the doubleness that lives at the core of everything human. Faith includes pain. Without closing its eyes to the risks of existence, it puts its own existence at risk. It can do that because, at that very same moment, it also includes grace, forgiveness, reconciliation, and liberation—everything that gives a special sense of recognition: this must be the way that life was actually meant to be.

Maybe it is at these moments that the pace of our heartbeats is most in harmony with God's love. The believer who lives in such trust finds in this trust the liberation to do the good. The moral driving force rests neither in any striving for reward nor in any fear of punishment.

The philosopher Friedrich Nietzsche (1844–1900) remarked sarcastically that Christians would need to look more saved if they were to make him believe in their Savior. Nietzsche had a point. If salvation never leads to bright eyes and happy smiles, something must be wrong somewhere! Christians who choose to dwell under the cross can forget the need to perform a dance of joy in front of the empty tomb.

Of course faith has something to do with our longing for happiness. Religion fills a deeply felt need in people—not only for safety and trust but also for joy and hopeful anticipation. "You, the morning sun who shines for ever . . . You, the open gate to bliss, give us hope and happiness" as one of the Church of Sweden *Kyries* goes. Spiritual commitment and religious activities can have good effects on people's well-being.

But even though faith can mobilize major forces in the fight against evil, it does not automatically lead to harmony and increased happiness. Well-being might be both positively and negatively affected.

Tribulations, doubts, temptations, and struggle are all part of the spiritual journey. And so is the experience of peace and new possibilities. During mass we wish one another the peace of God, well aware that this peace always and everywhere is both a threatened possibility and a liberating reality.

Liberation to do good is both a task and a gift. From our perspective, it requires both our will and our work—to distinguish the roles that evil plays in a complex world, to mobilize resistance, to act in the service of reconciliation. But authentic liberation also includes an inevitable element of gift. In spite of the knowledge of the ambiguity that is embedded at the core of everything human, we dare to be frank because we can count on God's lifegiving power to achieve something in and through us. Here the words of Paul in Philippians 2:12–13, which seem so self-contradictory, fit in well: "Work out your own salvation with fear and trembling, for it is God who is at work in you, enabling you both to will and to work for his good pleasure." The double starting point in the gift and the task enables a rest and a trust, even when the challenges and obstacles seem insurmountable.

And we certainly have more than enough challenges before us. To be set free for the good requires a good action plan. Here are some suggestions.

We need to take in facts and knowledge from numerous different fields. We need to clarify for ourselves and one another where we gain the orientation from for our moral compass. We need value-based leadership.

Besides knowledge of facts and morals, we need to strive for wisdom. That includes seeking to gain insight into the short- and long-term consequences of what we do or do not do, to work toward a righteous sharing of burdens and profits, to act with responsibility and transparency, to recognize our own mortality, and to become aware of how we bear our own suffering and of how we relate to the sufferings of other people.

We need to build trust between individuals, social groups, nations, and continents. Not least will the relationships that are burdened by much suspicion (like the one between Africa and Europe) become decisive for how we deal with global crises in the future.

We need imagination as an alternative to a culture of fear because, as Kierkegaard has said, anxiety over sin generates sin. We need that realism that sees mistakes, forgiveness, and reconciliation as real possibilities.

We need the right kind of empathy and compassion—not the kind of compassion that only confirms weakness, but the compassion that reacts with empathy and passion to other people's conditions of life so that they will be empowered to escape the grip of evil—and to live a life that is as wholesome as possible.

We need moral courage and a will to make sacrifices.

Moralizing can be very demoralizing. What is needed is a morality that has the capacity to liberate and to strengthen our deepest will and desire to be good and to do good. The world needs prayer and action to become one.

There is a liberating symbolism in the fact that churches traditionally have been built in an east-west direction. We come in from the west, the direction of sunset, transience, and the approaching darkness. We walk toward the east, the direction of sunrise and new opportunities. There is the altar, the center of the common meal of reconciliation in the presence of the risen Jesus, who gives humanity new opportunities of life. This walk from the west to the east might seem insignificant, but in the fight against evil it is an inexorable exercise. It can set us free for the good.

5

Be Grounded in Grace, Create in the World

The woman is highly educated and well-traveled. She does research and teaches at a Swedish university. Her upbringing and her education bear the stamp of secular Sweden. Recently, she has visited southeast Asia. She speaks of her surprise about how strongly the events of life there were embedded in rituals that seemed to be present everywhere. It made her feel strange but also a little envious, since it gave life an obvious sounding board. She asked, Now that we have got rid of so much that was holy in the past, what do we have to ground ourselves in?

Yes, what do we have to ground ourselves in? "Be grounded in grace, create in the world" became the basic motif that emerged when the Diocese of Lund in the Church of Sweden formulated a vision for the work of the church. It expresses the characteristics of a Christian community, and particularly of a church that stands in the Lutheran tradition, as the Church of Sweden does. *Be grounded in grace, create in the world* stands for continuity with our historical identity, while there is, at the same time, a critical edge. This formulation runs against anything that makes the church superficial and reduces parish life into an exclusively internal matter.

Be Grounded in Grace

Grace is a word that is alive both inside and outside the church. A blog analysis showed that the use of this word is not limited to the churchy corner of the internet but also turns up in more general contexts. People complain that there is too little grace in this world, and they long for more grace in life. Most people seem to have an understanding somewhere of what grace is, or at least a sense that grace is good for life. Otherwise the absence of grace would not have been noted with regret.

The Latin word for grace is *gratia*. From that we have the word *gratuitous*. Grace is something that we receive gratuitously, free of charge. Life is a gift before it becomes a task. This is particularly true about us as human beings. Compared to the offspring of animals, human babies are born remarkably helpless. Our dramatic and comparatively long-term dependence on the care of others before we can manage anything by ourselves is a reminder that we live by what we are given more than by what we do. Grace comes before our achievements and makes them possible. Grace comes to us so that we may be able to live our lives gracefully!

To be grounded is a corporeal experience. It means to feel firm ground under our feet in the midst of the waves. If I know that I can stand on firm ground, it is easier to allow myself to be exposed to the power of the wind and the waves. I may lose my footing for a while and float on the waves, but I know that I can soon reach the ground again. To be grounded means to have a foundation for my existence, to have my footing on the ground of existence. The theologian Paul Tillich

(1886–1965) used the phrase "the ground of being" as another term for God. In that sense, to be grounded in grace also means to be able to find rest in God.

But the image of an inexhaustible sea of grace does not only give positive associations. Isn't water both a source of life and a death-bringing force? And how can we be grounded in something that is endless?

Of course water both gives life and takes life. The broken, dry ground in drought-stricken Africa appears to be lifeless and speaks of death wherever water is lacking. Then, when the life-giving drops arrive, the power of growth is released in seeds that have been resting in the earth for years. Destruction in the wake of a tsunami speaks of the killing force of water. When water is stirred up by the forces of nature, it is often followed by death and chaos.

The same doubleness applies even to the water of baptism. The water of baptism releases the power of growth in a new life in union with Christ. At the same time, it is the place where, according to Martin Luther (1483–1546), the "old Adam" constantly needs to be drowned. That is how he spoke about that within us that opposes the life for which we are intended.

The symbolism of life and death connected with the water of baptism will emerge even more prominently in the future. We can hardly deal with the water of baptism without being aware that the uneven availability of water in the world is the reason behind great needs and catastrophes that will create unrest and conflicts of global dimensions.

Water can mean both life and death. A right attitude to water therefore presupposes both respect and trust. A lack of respect as well as a lack of trust can lead to dire consequences.

It is the same with the sea of grace. As it says in the hymn "Amazing Grace," "'Twas grace that taught my heart to fear, and grace my fears released. How precious did that grace appear the hour I first believed." Here too the doubleness appears: a lack of respect for grace is just as misleading as a lack of trust in grace.

God's will is for life. This is very serious. Things will go wrong if we only speak of water as the blue sea or as a nice-scented bubble bath. Water does not allow itself to be reduced to romanticism or wellness, even though it has an important role in that as well! Things will go just as wrong if we reduce God or God's grace to a little gold lining or to our own well-being as such. God's grace is so much greater. That is what holiness means. The holy includes both fear and fascination, as the theologian Rudolf Otto (1869–1937) wrote. We should fear and love God, Martin Luther wrote in his Catechism (1529), and he meant precisely that, taken together, deep respect and bold trust build up good relationships. That applies to our relationship to water as well as to God and to God's grace.

Now, if grace is inexhaustible, like an endless sea, how can you be grounded in it? You cannot be grounded in the middle of the open sea. It is close to the shore that people can find firm ground under their feet. There are of course shallow coastal areas where we can be grounded hundreds of meters out to sea. There are coasts where the tide makes it possible to walk for several miles on the seabed at low water. But no, we cannot be grounded in the middle of the sea. It is in the landscape of the shore that we find our life environment, our habitat.

We live in the border land where opposites meet: sea and land, grace and no grace, passion and indifference, eternity and time, life and death. We are not made to be grounded where there is only one thing as far as the eye can see. We are created in order to be grounded where the opposites meet, where currents break against each other, where sometimes fog and sometimes sparkling clarity is born. Our habitat is both-and rather than either-or. History is full of examples of how wrong things can go when people deny this life condition of the both-and and seek to create a culture of uniformity or purity in which only one absolute truth is permitted.

Create in the World

The relationship between the church and "the world" can look very different at different times and in different places. In Sweden, church and society used to be so mutually integrated that the Church of Sweden could be perceived as an expression of the nation. Now, when that belongs to history, the church is facing other alternatives. One possibility is a strictly spiritual self-understanding; another would be the setting up of some kind of parallel society that would pretend to be spiritual but would in fact only copy the state's exercise of power. Traces of both these attitudes can currently be observed in the Church of Sweden as well as in other faith communities. Both ways have their risks. Concentration on spirituality can walk hand in hand with a minimal interest in societal issues. And where the church's commitment in and for the world is weak, there is a threat of increasing superficiality with regard to faith and tradition. The church can become far too inward-looking: it can become a circle of people who enjoy being together, ending up in the entertainment business rather than in the challenge business. It may also be tempted to declare an earlier form of expression of the Christian faith to be the timeless "classic ideal," thus other earlier and contemporary expressions of faith would be suppressed to the detriment of the fullness of Christian testimony.

The model of the church as a parallel society is clearly expressed in the organizational costume churches like the Church of Sweden wear today and, for understandable reasons, is marked by reminiscences from the period when these churches were established national churches or state churches. What the old term "folk church" could possibly stand for in a new age must be reconsidered. The result of that reconsideration will have major significance for a church's self-understanding and for the way in which it will be perceived in today's and tomorrow's society.

Essentially, the church is an alternative community that finds its energy in the promise of the reign of God while it is at the same time deeply involved in realizing, in an anticipatory way, the good opportunities of life in this world.

It is good if we see a church that wants to be "a

thirsty underdog" rather than "a satisfied authority." It is good if the Church of Sweden wants to be less of an authority and more of a church, and less the Church of *Sweden* and more part of the global church in the twenty-first century.

Such a church does not represent any authoritarian claims to power, nor is it appeasing. In the words of the theologian Werner G. Jeanrond (b. 1955), it helps its members in an active participation in God's creative and innovative project. This happens through knowledge and practice of a way of living that leads to love for other people and for the rest of creation, to responsibility and care, to prayer and the profession of faith, to fasting and feasting, to discipline and contemplation.

Human creativity in the world has never been as prominent as it is now. Science and technology have moved the horizon for human creativity beyond the horizon of the earth. We know that our "creating" is so powerful that it can lead to the eradication of life on this planet. We have become aware of evolution and its history. And more than that, we even see opportunities to intervene in our own evolution. With this before his eyes, the theologian Philip Hefner (b. 1932) has described human beings as "created cocreators."

Our task is to birth the future that is most wholesome for the nature that has birthed us.

The choice of the word *cocreator* for human beings may seem controversial, since God's creating activity is unique and different in relation to all human creativity. At the same time, it cannot be denied that human beings actually are creative beings. The phrase "created cocreator" captures humanity's situation very well. Human beings are creators, and yet they are creation: radically dependent and interdependent. Human beings are creators who are cocreators: they are called to make their creative powers available for God's creating and innovative project. As created cocreators, we share responsibility for God's beloved world.

In our day and age, this responsibility is expressed in the environmental work and concern for climate justice, among other ways. This work consists of resolute programs as much as of thought, reflection, and prayer. Buildings must be heated, land and forests managed—here is both room and need for innovative thinking. This provides new openings for collaboration across religious boundaries. It is exciting that we can talk about "the greening of the world's religions": the world religions are becoming "green." Nature, or creation, plays a major role in the ideas of many religions: in the relationships between creator and creation in Judaism, Christianity, and Islam; in the cycle of matter in Hinduism and Jainism; in the emphasis on the mutual interdependence of all living beings in Buddhism; in the importance of the way through nature in Taoism and Confucianism. In spite of this, many religions have concentrated more on the salvation of the individual and on the life hereafter than on the integrity of creation. In parts of the American religious right, a certain kind of apocalyptic thinking has directly counteracted any positive commitment on behalf of the environment and the climate. In simple terms, the earth will perish anyway—the sooner the better, because then Jesus will return. It is only in recent years that politically influential evangelical Christians have begun to think in terms of ecological sustainability.

You might think that it should not have taken so long. Already in 1967, an article in *Science,* by the historian Lynn White Jr. (1907–1987), caused major upheaval in the Christian world. White criticized the understanding of God's commission to humanity to reign over creation (Gen 1:28) as carte blanche to exploit the earth and its resources.

In the wake of this criticism, the idea of *stewardship* has gained greater prominence in theology and preaching. Rather than being lords of creation, we are stewards of something that we do not own. But maybe the idea of stewardship is not sufficiently radical? As creators, human beings do well to remember that we are created beings and that we are part of numerous systems of mutual interdependence. A perspective that is centered on the individual and sets human beings against (the rest of) creation must be replaced by an understanding of human beings as part of creation. Today we encounter creation primarily as a globalized world in which the ecological balance is severely threatened and in which ecology, economy, and social justice must walk hand in hand. We need a self-understanding that makes it clear to us that we are both a product of creation and God's cocreators—as a hymn has put it, "God, when you breathe across our earth it is renewed, its face is shining. . . . Deep inside us the light is trembling, the Spirit of creation" (The Swedish Hymnal 476).

Triune God

According to the Christian faith, God reveals Godself as

a Trinitarian mystery, as Father, Son, and Holy Spirit. This three-in-one Trinity or Tri-unity is also the foundation for the three parts (articles) of the creed. The first article is about God the Creator; the second is about the Son, the example and the savior; and the third is about the Spirit and its life-giving flows in and through the life of the church.

Theology, and thus the language of the church, is in continual development. During the period of rationalism, the Trinitarian concept of God was perceived almost as a burden. In an age that celebrates clear statements free of ambiguity and contradiction, it is hard to transmit an understanding of God as one in three or three in one. It is easier to speak of God as a fairly abstract idea. In an age when our thoughts are more occupied with complexity and relationships, that which a hundred years ago was a burden suddenly becomes a pure goldmine. Since the 1980s, theological work on the doctrine of the Trinity has had an upswing. The perception of God as a mystery of relationships is a necessary alternative to the idea of God as an autocrat.

Christian pedagogy has taken for granted for a long time that one should start with the creator and end with the Spirit. But is that always the best order? Faith in God as Creator was probably articulated once upon a time as the result of a number of other experiences of God. It was the result of people's experiences of God rather than a beginning or a presupposition of such experiences. For many people, maybe for most, the life of faith does not begin with the question about the creator but with experiences of existential worry or spiritual hunger, and with experiences of how that hunger is satisfied. From that perspective, the third article offers a more obvious entrance than the first.

"Faith in supernatural powers and explanations is something that unites all religious people. It also implies setting boundaries for the search for truth." Thus wrote the author and atheist P. C. Jersild (b. 1935) (see chap. 3). Statements of this kind do not agree with the self-understanding of many believers. It is hard to recognize oneself in the claim that supernatural explanations would be the core of the faith. The primary criterion of faith is trust, not the acceptance of things that militate against reason. Religion is first and foremost a relationship. It is a way of relating to oneself and to other people, to the rest of creation and to the experience of the holy that has touched human beings as far back as we know. The claim that this would set boundaries for the search for truth feels like an alien thought. On the contrary, faith encourages that search and conversations about it. The main stream of Christian theology does not have identification of supernatural forces and the delivery of supernatural explanations as its goal. It is rather about a language for God's address and for the experiences of God that people have in the midst of progressing natural and social processes.

"Statements about God are meaningless, since I do not consider that God exists and cannot be explained. Statements about a smartphone are however meaningful, because I can explain it." This is an argument by a self-appointed rationalist. Wait a minute, I respond. There are very few people who can explain a smartphone, but there are very many who have experience of a smartphone. And it is not the explanation but the experiences that make it meaningful to talk about it. There are very few people who would attempt to explain God and the mystery of the holy, but there are all the more people who have experience of God—experiences of God's presence and of God's absence. That is what makes the conversation meaningful.

There are moments when the words "God, how wonderful!" cannot be stopped. And there are moments when we cannot resist the cry, "God, my God, why have you forsaken me?" In such moments reasoning about the existence or non-existence of God will not add much meaning. That does not make such reasoning superfluous. It has been undertaken many times throughout the history of theology and still offers fascinating reading for anyone who is interested in philosophy and theology. But regardless of the various fates of these so-called proofs of God, many people have, and continue all the time to have, experiences of faith, trust, mistrust, longing, search, and healing.

Faith cannot make do without discussions about a concept of God. At the same time, it is rarely there that existential decisions are made. When we long for salvation, blessedness, and being grounded in grace, it is perhaps not a concept of God that we are searching for in the first place but rather an encounter with a God before whom we can sing and dance and even get on our knees in adoration.

In Matthew 28 we meet the commission to baptize and to engage in mission in order to make all people disciples, to baptize them in the name of the Father, the Son, and the Holy Spirit, and to teach them to keep all the commandments that Jesus has given us. To win disciples is about inspiring learning and gathering people together in hope. At the center, there is baptism as the foundation for the church's identity and action. And to keep the commandments is part of meeting the challenges of life and of the world.

Learning and Hope

Inspiration is linked to the Spirit. Learning and renewal carry the signature of the Holy Spirit. Learning has always been very important in the Lutheran tradition. The Bible in the vernacular, catechism, the promotion of schools—the Reformation was a popular education movement that started on a university campus. Even though the new thinking became rigid, and the teaching could degenerate into authoritarian methods of handing down tradition, the basic idea remains: the knowledge that I have provides freedom. The person who knows his or her catechism by heart has in principle won the tools for living as a free citizen. That was the thinking.

As I have shown in chapter 2, we live in an age when secularization coincides with the return of religion to a greater degree of visibility. Precisely for that reason, the need for teaching, discovery, and exploration of the Christian tradition and its cultural heritage is increasing. The church provides a unique space for conversations that may be difficult to have in any other place in society. A church building provides room for addressing people in a way that is difficult or impossible elsewhere. That which in another context might be perceived as negative provocation can become a positive challenge in a church.

Over the years that I have been a bishop, I have often met people who are deeply grateful for what the church's adult education called catechumenate has given them in terms of knowledge, spiritual deepening, fellowship, and the ability to engage in conversations about their faith. I hope that the number of catechumenate groups that gather women and men from different age groups will continue to grow. In a good and much-longed-for way, that kind of exploration of faith and life can also break age segregation, which is so common in society, and which we in the church have adopted in rather flagrant ways.

Another need that is increasing in our age is the necessity for dialogue with all people of good will, regardless of their faith. Movements such as Religions for Peace and the Parliament of the World Religions have taken on a role that is becoming increasingly important. Even dialogue with politics, literature, art, culture, and the sciences remain urgent. Different areas of knowledge should be able to converge in the church. All important issues have a home here. We need a spirit of curiosity and openness, always with opportunities for reflection and maybe criticism on the basis of a Christian view of life. There is often not just one specific Christian attitude. The advice in 1 Thessalonians 5:19–22 must apply: "Do not quench the Spirit . . . but test everything; hold fast to what is good; abstain from every form of evil."

This is a matter of cultivating hope—not only for ourselves as individuals or as a small group. Hope is cultivated in pastoral care, in worship, in diaconal ministry, in teaching, and in everything else that takes place in and through a congregation.

Successful cultivation is a result of good interplay between human activity and matters that are not under our control. Knowledge and hard work are needed in order to create the best preconditions for growth. Attention is required throughout that process—the right moments for sowing, watering, fertilizing, thinning out, and harvesting must be awaited. Even so, we cannot force good results. Growth is always also a gift that must be awaited. Correspondingly, the cultivation of hope unites human work with

BE GROUNDED IN GRACE

the gifts of the Spirit. To cultivate hope for the world is part of the common life of the congregation. In the church, there should be a context in which we can lift up our eyes and look beyond our own limitations to the future.

The church is a fascinating community, even when looked at from the outside. God's lovingkindness toward imperfect, "ordinary" people is proclaimed untiringly. Sunday after Sunday, people persist in celebrating the victory of life over death and express their joy that they belong to God, to one another, and to the entire creation. Not to mention all the cultivation of hope that takes place in the weekday work.

God's people can primarily be described as a people of hope. Quite rightly, the author of 1 Peter encourages us: "Always be ready to make your defense to anyone who demands from you an account of the hope that is in you; yet do it with gentleness and reverence. Keep your conscience clear" (1 Pet 3:15–16). The empathy and the pride that speaks from this Bible passage is a good guiding principle for being the church in the twenty-first century.

Baptism as the Foundation

Baptism is the foundation for life as a Christian. It lays the foundation for the identity of the individual as a Christian and builds up the church as a community. At every baptism, the church becomes visible anew. Baptism constitutes the basis for living as a Christian—it is a lifelong relationship from which we never risk disqualifying ourselves, whatever evil might happen. Baptism is an expression of how we may confidently be grounded in God's grace through life and death.

Baptism is a very simple action that carries many strong motifs: a path to new birth (Titus 3:4–8), the way through death to life (Rom 6:3–4), belonging to Jesus Christ (Rom 6:5), incorporation into the body of Christ and the community of the church (1 Cor 12:27), church unity (Eph 4:5; Col 3:15), repentance and forgiveness (Acts 2:38), to be clothed with Christ (Gal 3:27), equality (Gal 3:28), grace (Rom 5:2; Eph 2:8), commission (Matt 28:18–20; John 17:18). In baptism, everything is given to us gratuitously, free of charge, by grace. Access to baptism must therefore be generous. That applies theologically as well as in a practical sense. Baptism should be easily available to people of all ages.

Our vocation to live courageously, in trust and love,

with Jesus as our model, rests on baptism. There is a great promise connected with baptism. The apostle Paul writes in Romans 6:4 about a new quality of life that reaches beyond our life on this earth: "Therefore we have been buried with him by baptism into death, so that, just as Christ was raised from the dead by the glory of the Father, we too might walk in newness of life."

In baptism we make ourselves dependent on grace—maybe the only dependence that gives perfect freedom. It is said that when Martin Luther was beset by insecurity and doubts, he took a piece of chalk and wrote on the table in front of himself, "I have been baptized in the name of Jesus." That is one way to be grounded in grace!

All forms of activities in the church are linked to baptism. It is either about accompanying children, women, and men who might be on their way toward baptism, or about supporting the baptized in their life in baptism. Baptism therefore merits greater prominence in our own life as well as in the life and work of the church.

The kinship of all the baptized becomes clear in the worldwide church and in international and ecumenical friendships between congregations and dioceses in different parts of the world. In the church, baptism has a greater validity than the passport! The church is always "glocal"—both global and local. It constitutes a community in which the members carry one another in prayer and intercession. Life in baptism is the very opposite of envy and bullying. It inspires us to see, accept, and develop one another's gifts. It also means that the congregation should function as a welcoming community, turned outward and prepared to welcome new members. Active recruitment to membership and mission is part of the life of baptism.

Baptism has an obvious link to the life of worship. Just as our breathing in and out sustains the life of our body, so the life of baptism consists of gathering and sending. The Eucharist is a concentrated expression of this: to be gathered for a meal in communion with Jesus Christ and with one another, and to be sent out from the altar into the life in the world.

Sometimes hesitations arise about how far the church might dare to highlight baptism. Would it become exclusive for the non-baptized? At a time when we are keen to combat discrimination, this is an issue that must be taken seriously. The laudable ambition to expose even hidden discrimination also has a backside, namely the risk of seeing discrimination where it does not exist, and to legitimize feelings of being offended even when they are built on a misunderstanding.

The emphasis on baptism is not exclusive, as long as it is clear that it is an act of God's grace, which does not require anything in return. "Look, here is water! What is to prevent me from being baptized?" the Ethiopian eunuch asked in Acts 8:36 after a minimum of preparation. And the preacher Philip did not hesitate to baptize him. In that sense baptism is the most inclusive act anyone can imagine. It is only if you assume that "non-baptized" is an irrevocable state that baptism would become exclusive. The (as-yet) non-baptized person who finds the way to a church should of course be met by welcoming care and learn how they—if they so wish—can grow into full participation in the Christian community. It is not about manifesting an either-or (either believer or non-believer) but about a process of maturing in which, for various reasons, we have reached different stages.

A church with baptism at the center must question and change a pattern that currently characterizes much of what we do, that is, the consumerist pattern. *Homo sapiens* has after all been around far longer than *homo consumentus!* We miss our goal if we define the church primarily through employees who offer services and programs to interested participants. To be the church is not about some people producing religious experiences that can be consumed by members (and to some extent by non-members). To be the church is more than delivering nice get-togethers. A nice atmosphere is often a side effect of good work, but for church workers, a nice atmosphere cannot be a goal in itself.

Good service, openness, and accessibility must be self-evident. So also the awareness that for many members, good service is just about the only expectation they have of their church. But our mission as a church is greater than that. The church has never been able to live through its professional Christians only. God gathers a people of women, men, and children who through baptism are called and empowered to live as Christians, to be grounded in grace and to create in the world.

This is what made Martin Luther speak of the priesthood of all believers. In the strength of their baptism, all Christians have a vocation, regardless of what their everyday work is. Church professionals have the task of helping people to live out this vocation in their daily life. To live out your vocation can sometimes be controversial, or it can attract attention, but most of the time it happens without much recognition. Life in the everyday "plod-on" in baptism is often not glamourous, even though it might happen at the cost of a serious inner struggle. When the new person—the person who, according to Luther's Small Catechism, "every day emerges and rises"—in baptism is victorious over temptations to give in to the less-good alternatives, then life usually just carries on as normal. Anything remarkable rarely happens. The theologian Gustaf Wingren (1910–2000) has illustrated this through a picturesque but evocative example. "If a baptized person runs a sausage stall, he will have numerous opportunities secretly to combat the temptation to earn money from bad food. If he manages to conquer the temptation, the result will not always show up in the book-keeping as a triumphal cry: 'The church is selling excellent sausages!' It is quite sufficient that the customers become satisfied without falling ill. What it is about is what is best for the *neighbor*."

Wingren continued with another example: the sea captain who is tempted to dump oil in the sea when not noticed. If the "old" person is victorious, millions of people, animals, and plants may be affected. If the "new" person is victorious, hardly anything will be noticed along the coasts. In that way even the normal daily events are a real wonder of creative power (Ps 104:27–30).

But even when things go wrong, and the "old" person wins over the "new," the gift of baptism remains. Life in baptism is grounded in grace. It is always possible to return to that which God by grace has given us. Prayer, pastoral care, and confession can make that very concrete and specific for us.

In a church that highlights the life in baptism, the leaders and staff will work more strategically. The purpose must be less about serving ready-cooked food and more about enabling and supporting people in their growth in the Christian life as good stewards of God's multi-colored grace. The goal for church work is not to make people committed to the groups of the church but to give them the impetus and skill to live a Christian life—to be salt and light (Matt 5:13–16)—in the various contexts of which each one of us are part. Our task as a church is to liberate sociability (see chap. 1) but not to monopolize it. The pulse of the church beats to the rhythm of gathering and sending as it is expressed in our worship: the gathering, praise and confession, the Word, the sacraments, and the sending.

Is the congregation a home? It is, in the sense that the congregation should be like open arms to which people are welcome as they are—a place where you do not have to pretend anything. Those arms should not close around people but should now and then become a friendly but firm pat on the back: now go and live out what you participate in when we celebrate the Eucharist. In the *Kyrie*, the "Lord have mercy," you express all your anxiety, need, and lament. In the *Gloria*, the song of praise, you express thanksgiving, joy, and love. The confession of sin opens for you to receive forgiveness and healing and new opportunities; the Bible readings and the sermon challenge, bring comfort, and give guidance. In the *Credo*, the profession of the faith of the church, and in the Lord's Prayer (the "Our Father"), it becomes clear that our personal relationship to God is embedded in a common tradition across time and space. We are reminded that we have been baptized in order to live in communion with God, with one another, and with the whole of creation. In the sharing of the bread that has sprung forth from the earth and in the drink from the vine, it is not only the memory of the life, death, and victory over death of Jesus that becomes alive. In the Eucharist is realized the community of justice that we are still lacking in this world. At the communion table, there is no difference between people. That trains us in ways of treating each other that are not defined by purchasing power, by designer clothes, by residence address, by gender, by profession, or by nationality. At the communion table, we are constantly reminded that we actually live more by what we have been given than by what we do. We live by grace.

It might work on the television, but very rarely in real life, that some professionals equip a home perfectly and then expect a family to move in and immediately feel at home. Homes are built in, through, and during the progress of life. So too God creates, in, through, and during the natural and social processes as they are going on. The same applies to the church as a home.

To Meet the Challenges of Life and of the World

There is no lack of challenges in our lives and in our world. I have already said that our habitat is not an unambiguous landscape but a borderland of coastal landscapes in which various elements and streams meet. Ambiguity and doubleness exist both in our exterior and our interior environments (see chap. 4). The deep doubleness at the core of everything human gives us experiences of disappointment, failure, and evil. It is, however, not only moral shortcomings that confront us with heavy thoughts. Even the course of nature faces us with questions about meaning. Why is there so much cruelty in nature? Why has the long history of evolution been accompanied by suffering and death? Is the history of suffering in fact universal? Is there a cosmic passion history that we contemplate when, during Lent, we "go up to Jerusalem" (Swedish Hymnal 135) with Jesus? The cross in the midst of the universe (Swedish Hymnal 438) claims that the death of Christ on the cross has cosmic significance. As Christians, we believe that the cosmic history is crossed through and illuminated by an even more passionate passion: God's love for the world.

We are challenged by both wealth and need, within us and around us, and by the commandment to love God and our neighbor as ourselves—well aware that to love ourselves in the right way can be the most difficult love of all. It is therefore important to constantly highlight new opportunities. It is a great benefit to be able to make use of our freedom to begin anew, again and again, since there is the possibility of forgiveness and reconciliation. It is indeed an art to be a human being!

In diaconal ministry, prayer, conversation, and action, the church should be an instrument of the realm of God. In order to be that, it is not enough to have employed members of the church. The church functions as an instrument of the realm of God wherever a baptized person lives his or her life in accordance with his or her vocation. Success and failure in this are no mere trifles. What we do or don't do has consequences, locally as well as globally.

Singing and music have a special role in motivating us and strengthening our powers of good will. Music in various forms is indispensable in the formation and handing on of the songs of faith and the language of prayer. Luther himself considered music the only form of art that is equal to theology since, like theology, it gives a calm and happy heart. The devil—the father of sad worries and anxious wanderings—takes flight, according to Luther's late-medieval way of looking at existence, at the voice of music, just as he does at the words of theology.

It might well be true that more people have been sung than preached into the realm of God. It is hard to imagine a church without a choir and the life of music.

BE GROUNDED IN GRACE

In Lutheran churches, the common singing of hymns usually plays a significant role. The songs, texts, and prayers gathered in hymnals represent a great cultural wealth, and a hymnal is an asset for individual devotions—not only as a book of songs but as a book to read as well.

Some words from a hymn from the 1970s speak of the will to meet the challenges of life and of the world: "make something new, something burning of us, lead us to build a world of justice—action and prayer may be one" (Swedish Hymnal 292). ("Asking that we may be led and enabled, truly united to build new communities, worship and work must be one" [Worship the Lord, text Fred Kaan, 1972].)

To live with changes is part of the challenges of life and of the world. We know that the answers of today will be tested by the questions of tomorrow. That may apply even to our best answers. A radical and deep openness is therefore needed. As the church, we need to become forerunners; we need to find sustainable ways to communicate in multicultural societies. That is one among many ways of being the church in critical solidarity with society.

The world of the future will probably be more Asian than Western, more female than male, more colored than white, more mixed, more uneven, and less well-fed than we are generally prepared to imagine. Vulnerability at the level of the individual, the community, and the system will not become any lesser. The needs for good leadership will increase rather than decrease. To meet the challenges of life and of the world is to a great extent about this: knowing that God is greater than our best achievements and our worst failures, we can liberate one another to do what is good.

God Is Greater

In the borderland that is our human habitat, grace and no-grace meet. Time meets eternity, and the ambiguity in everything human is apparent. It is an environment in which questions often become precisely questions about borders and limits. As such, they merit particular attention because the questions we ask and have to face when we reach borders are often essential. They often concern who we are deep down and where we ultimately belong.

Between 2001 and 2007, I lived with questions of borders in quite a specific way. I traveled a lot between Europe and the United States, where I lived and worked at that time. Entry into the United States was

BE GROUNDED IN GRACE

full of surprises every time—sometimes strange border questions were asked. Some were kinder than others. Some were worth thinking about more than others.

Once, when I had landed at Chicago O'Hare, the immigration officer looked at my papers and said, "So you are a theologian. Tell me, what is the basic principle in theology?" Since my students did not usually ask me just that, I had to think for a moment, and then I answered, "God."

He continued, "So you are teaching at the *Lutheran* School of Theology at Chicago. That has something to do with that Martin Luther, doesn't it?"

"Of course," I said.

"Was it not he who talked in the sixteenth century about justification by grace through faith?" Quite impressed by this unexpected knowledge, I said, "You are absolutely right."

The officer bored further, "What does it mean, then—justified by grace through faith?" By then the line behind me had grown considerably, so it was not the moment for any longer exposition. I said, "It means: you get your vacation first, and then you get to work, out of sheer joy and love, sort of."

He seemed satisfied, but only for a second, for then he came back to it again. "If it says that in the Bible, why did it take 1,500 years before Luther discovered that?" I tried to suggest that it was probably a rediscovery rather than a discovery, but the question hung in the air long after I had left the immigration control behind on that day.

If the basic principle of faith is as simple as three letters—G-O-D, God—why is it that after several thousands of years, we still do not have all the answers? And why is it that we can be fairly sure that today's answers will be revised by tomorrow's questions? If the basic principle of faith is as simple as three letters, why is it that we must try, again and again, to find new words for what we mean by putting our trust in God and for what it means to be a Christian? It is because God is always greater.

"By this we will know that we are from the truth and will reassure our hearts before him whenever our hearts condemn us; for *God is greater* than our hearts, and he knows everything," it says in 1 John 3:19–20 (emphasis added). It easily happens that our heart condemns us. Sometimes it happens for good and serious reasons, because we have done wrong in one way or another. But quite often it happens on false grounds, because someone has made us believe that we are embarrassing, that we don't fit in, that we are insuf-

BE GROUNDED IN GRACE

ficient, or that we have made fools of ourselves. It also happens that it is we ourselves who tell ourselves this, but it is often other voices that force our attention in a way or to an extent that they ought not to do.

With regard to the effect, it doesn't matter very much whether we condemn ourselves for good or bad reasons. The result is always equally destructive: we lose something of our openness and spontaneity; we close up within ourselves; we become curved in on ourselves as the same Martin Luther described it. In that situation the gospel, the good news, says, "God is greater than all this." God understands the good and the bad reasons and much more than that. God understands everything. God lets us loose from being curved in on ourselves so that we can live with a straight back and open arms so that, as the first letter of John also says, we can love in action and in truth. That is what the story of Jesus is about.

God is greater than our heart—that gives us comfort, hope, and confidence. To rest in the assurance that "God is greater" than both my best and my worst means to have peace in the midst of all the anxiety that the world and our own hearts can cause us. The God who is greater than our heart, and who understands everything, is worthy of our trust and confidence. But God is a God of surprises. Sometimes God also stands for unease in the midst of our ease. God is greater than our images of God. However much we know, and however strong our faith is, we will never be done with all answers, and we will never possess everything.

And we certainly know quite a lot. The treasure of knowledge and wisdom that humanity has gathered throughout the centuries is fantastic: art and erudition in every form, scientific knowledge and technological opportunities that are amazing when they are at their best. And precisely when everything is at its best, self-sufficiency and conceit is also very close at hand. The history of humanity is full of painful examples. In the name of religion, politics, science, or of our own culture, totalitarian claims have been raised that have led to persecution of people and things that are different.

The phrase "God is greater" questions all claims that pretend to be ultimate truth. And it does so in a very healthy way. Because if God is always greater than the very best that we can achieve, then we will do well to leave a door ajar for better learning; then it is right to seek conversation with the person who is different; then it is important that we persevere in respect for one another and in trustful prayer for the Holy Spirit of truth. The world in which we live, and the questions that humanity is facing, make this absolutely necessary.

God is greater. So great that God can be in all things, from the greatest to the smallest—in the mystery of the Milky Way as well as in the elementary particles that travel through our bodies. A sense of wonder is spot on! A sense of awe and wonder before God, who is greater, can make us feel small in a special way. When the powers of bureaucracy spread awe and wonder around themselves, human beings often feel reduced and react with a sense of being powerless or with anger. A sense of awe and wonder before the God who is greater is different. It can make me feel small in a grand way, in a way that does not diminish our dignity as humans but, on the contrary, strengthens it.

The story of Jesus corrects our sense of proportions. When our thoughts are too small, we are provoked by Jesus to think greater thoughts. When we are thinking too highly, Jesus challenges us to meet God in the least and most insignificant people. It is the work of the Holy Spirit to keep the questions alive, particularly those border questions that are about who we are and where we belong. If God is greater, there is every reason to worship so that we can rejoice in belonging together with God, with one another, and with the whole of creation. Then it is meaningful that people gather together in a church that inspires learning and transmits hope on the basis of baptism in order to meet the challenges of life and of the world. Then it is also meaningful that the church becomes and remains a context in which people can continue to be in constant dialogue with one another, with society at large, and with brothers and sisters in the faith who belong to other parts of the church or to other religions. God is greater. Greater than what? Where this book ends, it is my hope that new conversations and further reflections will begin.

Questions for Reflection and Conversation

By Marlene Holmqvist, Sensus Study Association

Critical Solidarity

1. What are your thoughts about the statement, "The place of the church is in the midst of the world" in light of sociability?

2. How private is religion really? How neutral should we be, where, and when?

3. In what way can the church take social responsibility?

4. The UN Convention on the Rights of the

QUESTIONS FOR REFLECTION AND CONVERSATION

> Child lays down children's right to spiritual development. How do we help children with this in the best way? Key concepts: indoctrination, information, education, nurture.

5. How great an importance should religion be allowed to have in a society?

6. Is a democratic society necessarily secular? Key concepts: democracy, secularization, sect, indoctrination, confession, religious illiteracy.

7. How important is "rank-and-file" ecumenism?

8. Discuss the importance of interreligious dialogue.

Your Own Reflections and Thoughts

....
....
....
....

QUESTIONS FOR REFLECTION AND CONVERSATION

After Secularization

1. Is it meaningful to speak of "the Christian West"? Why? Why not?

2. People are interested in spirituality, but there is great lack of knowledge about Christianity. How do we relate to that?

3. In what way could Lydia be a source of inspiration to us all?

4. How do we relate to the following concepts: "believing without belonging" and "belonging without believing"?

5. The author notes the influence of postmodern thought, in which explanations and "truths" must be seen in a historic context, and the question is whether everything can be seen as constructions. What does the author think, and what do you yourself think?

Your Own Reflections and Thoughts

. . . .
. . . .

QUESTIONS FOR REFLECTION AND CONVERSATION

....
....

Beyond the Caricatures

1. How do we look at "the knowledge of faith" and our "faith in knowledge"?

2. Like the church father Tertullian, we could cry out, "What does Athens have to do with Jerusalem"? In other words, how do we consider the relationship between science and religion?

3. How important is it to engage in dialogue between different fields of knowledge, such as the natural sciences and theology?

4. Are metaphors needed? Why? Why not?

5. Is it possible to trust theology and the natural sciences? What are the arguments in favor and against?

6. Christian faith and Darwin's theory of evolution: How do they fit together?

7. Is God a figment of our brains? What is your reasoning?

QUESTIONS FOR REFLECTION AND CONVERSATION

8. The author writes, "God is a relationship of love and not a scientific hypothesis. The relationship of love includes a love of wisdom." What are your views of these thoughts?

Your Own Reflections and Thoughts

....
....
....
....

Cosmic Passion History

1. Do we live in a rational and controlled society in which we can reject evil as a concept?

2. How do you see the relationship between "natural evil" and "moral evil"?

3. Reflect on whether religious activity and cultural diversity are dangerous to society and/or enriching for the individual and for the collective whole.

4. How do you view the connection between religion and good actions?

QUESTIONS FOR REFLECTION AND CONVERSATION

5. How important is it to be able to forgive?
6. Why is it so important to be able to see one's own insufficiency and to have courage to look into the abyss?
7. How can we define "sin"?
8. How is it that quite ordinary people can commit really evil actions?
9. To set ourselves free for good actions, we need a good action plan. Discuss the author's suggestions toward the end of the chapter.

Your Own Reflections and Thoughts

....
....
....
....

Be Grounded in Grace, Create in the World

1. What is it in the Christian faith and community that provides the greatest support in your life?

QUESTIONS FOR REFLECTION AND CONVERSATION

2. What do you want to develop in the church?
3. What constitutes a good church?
4. What does "Be grounded in grace, create in the world" mean to you?
5. The author writes that "we live in an age when secularization coincides with the return of religion to a greater degree of visibility. Precisely for that reason, the need for teaching, discovery, and exploration of the Christian tradition and its cultural heritage is increasing." What are your views on that statement?
6. What does "God is greater" mean for us?

Your Own Reflections and Thoughts

....
....
....
....

Sources and References

Critical Solidarity

Mikael Mogren's chronicle mentioned on page 4 was published in *Svensk kyrkotidning* 4 (2008). Maciej Zaremba's series of articles *I väntan på Sverige*, mentioned on page 8, was published in 2009 in *Dagens Nyheter*. The graffiti in Rome mentioned on page 8 can be found on English Wikipedia. The information on page 11 about Swedish single women inseminated in Copenhagen is taken from *Sydsvenskan,* September 29, 2009, 11 (the A part). The quotation from *Kyrkoordning för Svenska kyrkan* on page 17 is taken from the introduction to part 1: "Svenska kyrkan som evangelisk-luthersk trossamfund." The quotation by Emilie M.

SOURCES AND REFERENCES

Townes on page 24 is taken from the periodical *Christian Century*, June 29, 2010. The rule of thumb for interfaith dialogue on page 38 was inspired by the former Bishop of Stockholm and professor of Harvard University Krister Stendahl (1921–2008). Olle Nivenius's pastoral letter to the diocese of Lund, mentioned on page 38, was titled *Tjäna Herren med glädje*. It was published in 1970.

After Secularization

The reference to Jacques Delors originates from compilations of several speeches to the European churches during the 1990s, particularly in 1992, when Delors frequently mentioned the need to create a soul for Europe. It has reached the author through an article by Anton van Hooff, "Europa och den helige Benedictus" in the Swedish periodical *Signum* 4 (1995). The theme issue of *Der Spiegel* that is mentioned on page 50 was number 9 (2006), and that mentioned on page 51 was number 22 (2007). The quotation by Ylva Eggehorn on page 50 is taken from the periodical *NOD* 1 (2007):21. The quotation from *Sydsvenskan* on page 51 is taken from the article by Staffan Söderberg on page B4 (the cultural part) on November 19, 2007. Peter Sandberg made a statement in *Kyrkans Tidning*, and the quotation on page 51 is taken from the website edition. The press release from Sveriges Radio on the same page is taken from *Dagen*. The reviewer quoted on page 54 was Stefan Jonsson in *Dagens Nyheter,* October 7, 2007, 7, in the cultural part. The summary of Gianni Vattimo on page 70 is based on his contribution to the dialogue book *The Future of Religion* with Richard Rorty, ed. Santiago Zabala (2005). The reference to Jürgen Habermas on page 72 refers to Jürgen Habermas and Joseph Ratzinger's book *Dialektik der Säkularisierung*, 7th ed. (2007), 29–33. The quotations from *The Economist* on pages 74 and 75 are taken from https://tinyurl.com/y9p5jnjn. The quotation on page 73 from E. O. Wilson's book *The Creation: An Appeal to Save Life on Earth* is taken from *Religion & Ethics*. The quotation on page 73 is taken from the book *Re-Ordering Nature*, ed. Celia Deane-Drummond and Bronislaw Szerszynski with Robin Grove-White (2003), 22.

Beyond the Caricatures

The lecture in Oxford mentioned on page 77 was published in *Zygon: Journal of Religion and Science* 41, no. 4 (2006): 955–73. The quotation by P. C. Jersild on page

SOURCES AND REFERENCES

79 is taken from *Dagens Nyheter*, February 15, 2010, 5, in the cultural part. The investigations mentioned on page 79 have been reported in *Eurobarometer* 52, no. 1. The information on page 80 about the view of astrology as a science is reiterated in accordance with the barometer from Vetenskap & Allmänhet, November 2010. Among the periodicals in the field of the natural sciences and religion mentioned on page 84, the following are important: *Zygon: Journal of Religion and Science* and *Theology and Science*. Among centers for dialogue, the following can be mentioned: Center for Theology and the Natural Sciences (CTNS), Berkeley; Zygon Center for Religion and Science (ZCRS), Chicago; and the Ian Ramsey Centre for Science and Religion, Oxford. The European Society for the Study of Science and Theology (ESSSAT) organizes regular conferences. The quotation by Francis Bacon on page 89 is taken from *The Philosophy of Francis Bacon: An Essay on Its Development from 1603 to 1609 with New Translations of Fundamental Texts*, ed. Benjamin Farrington (1964), 62. The statement by the pope on page 91 is from page 13 of *Physics, Philosophy and Theology: A Common Quest for Understanding*, ed. Robert John Russell, William R. Stoeger, and George V. Coyne (1988). The quotations on page 93 from the book by Klaus Mainzer, *Symmetry*

SOURCES AND REFERENCES

and Complexity, are found on pages 23 and 272. The quotations by Alan Lightman on page 95 are taken from his book *A Sense of the Mysterious: Science and the Human Spirit* (2005), 49–50, 63–64. The reference to Emily Martin on page 95 is to her article in *The Science Studies Reader*, ed. Mario Biagioli (1999), 358–71. The quotation by Karl Barth on page 96 was originally translated from his book *Das Wort Gottes und die Theologie* (1929), 158, into Swedish. The English wording is quoted from *The Word of God and Theology*, trans. Amy Marga (2011). Information on page 100 on how the doctrine on evolution was received in different parts of the world comes from David Livingstone's contribution to the book *Envisioning Nature, Science, and Religion*, ed. James D. Proctor (2009), 103–30. Charles Darwin on page 104 is quoted from https://tinyurl.com/y8ab6s. The quotation on page 105 is in the Records by the American Congress from 1999, H4214 (June 14), H4366 (June 16) and H4671 (June 22). Information about the brain activities by people who meditate on page 107 is taken from Andrew Newberg, Eugene d'Aquili, and Vince Rause, *Why God Won't Go Away: Brain Science and the Biology of Belief* (2002). The quotations by Krister Stendahl on page 110 are taken from his book *Meanings: The Bible as Document and as Guide* (Fortress Press, 1984). The thoughts on page 111 about the physiological qualities of the soul have been reported according to Warren S. Brown's article in *Whatever Happened to the Soul? Scientific and Theological Portraits of Human Nature*, ed. Warren S. Brown, Nancey Murphy, and H. Newton Maloney (1998), 99.

Cosmic Passion History

Håkan Boström's article quoted on page 117 was printed on page 4 of *Dagens Nyheter,* August 4, 2009. The sermon I quote on page 119 was preached in the Church of Bollmoradalen, the Parish of Tyresö, on the Thursday after the murder of Olof Palme (March 6, 1986). The summary of Catherine Keller on page 123 is based on her contribution to the book *Christianity and Ecology: Seeking the Well-Being of Earth and Humans*, ed. Dieter T. Hessel and Rosemary Radford Ruether (2000), 183–98. Per Bak's thoughts about criticality and catastrophism on page 125 are reported according to his book *How Nature Works* (1996). The quotation on page 126 by Ursula Goodenough and Terrence W. Deacon is taken from their article "From Biology to Consciousness to Morality" in *Zygon* 28 (2003): 801–19. The quotation by George W. Bush on page 129 I have translated

SOURCES AND REFERENCES

from Al Gore's book *The Assault on Reason* (2007), which I have read in a German translation (2009). The reference to modern brain research on page 130 refers, for example, to Antonio Damasio's book *Descartes' Error: Emotion, Reason, and the Human Brain* (1999). The interview with Katri Linna mentioned on page 131 was published in *Kyrkans Tidning* 50 (2009). That the visit by the staff members of the American president (page 133) attracted media attention could be seen on the front page of the Melbourne newspaper *The Age,* December 10, 2009. The summary of Desmond Tutu on page 137 is based on his book *No Future without Forgiveness* (New York: Doubleday, 1999). The quotation on page 137 is found on page 86. The quotation on page 138 from Desmond and Mpho Tutu's book *Made for Goodness: And Why It Makes All the Difference in the World* (HarperCollins, 2010) is taken from page 150. Heiko Oberman's biography of Luther, which is mentioned on page 140, was published in 1982 with the title *Mensch zwischen Gott und Teufel*. The Kierkegaard quotation on page 141 is taken from *The Concept of Anxiety*, ed. and trans. Reidar Thome in collaboration with Albert B. Anderson (1980), 61, and the quotation on page 143 is found on page 155. The quotations from *Diapsalmata* on page 144 are taken from *Either/Or: A Fragment of Life*, ed. Victor Eremita, trans. Alastair Hannay (1992), 48, 56.

Be Grounded in Grace, Create in the World

Between 2007 and 2014 I was the bishop of the Diocese of Lund. During the spring of 2009 the diocesan governing body decided to work out a vision for the diocese (page 151). The purpose was to express the self-understanding of the Church of Sweden, its "core values," and to inspire, motivate, and hold together the work within the diocese. At an early stage a strong basic motif emerged that was sustained throughout the entire process: be grounded in grace, create in the world. These words were complemented during the progress of the work by the following three lines: inspire learning and gather around hope on the foundation of baptism in order to meet the challenges of life and of the world. In November 2010 the diocesan delegates expressed their support for this vision. Philip Hefner speaks of the mission of the human being as God's "created cocreator" (page 157) on page 27 of his book *The Human Factor* (1993). The article by Lynn White mentioned on page 158 was published under the title "The Historical Roots of Our Ecologic Crisis" in

SOURCES AND REFERENCES

Science 155, no. 3767 (1967): 1203–7. The quotation by P. C. Jersild on page 160 is taken from *Dagens Nyheter*, February 15, 2010. The quotation by Gustaf Wingren on page 167 is taken from *Gustaf Wingren: Människan och teologen* by Bengt Kristensson Uggla (2010), 198. Luther's praise of music on page 171 can be found in his letter to Ludwig Senfl, October 4, 1530, in Martin Luther, *Ausgewählte Schriften*, vol. 6, ed. Karin Bornkamm and Gerhard Ebeling, 2nd ed. (1983), 134. Biblical quotations have been taken from the New Revised Standard Version.